This book is a gift to anyone struggling wit[
Over 90 days, Mary shares wisdom from
walked in front of us. I expect this devotio[
ion to many in their healing journey.

—Richard Leakey, dir[

Mary DeMuth writes *Healing Every Day* from a "me too" perspective. She knows heartache, but she also knows hope. Take this 90-day journey with her, and experience renewal and refreshment that can only be found in Jesus Christ.

—Dr. Laurel Shaler, associate professor, director of Master of Arts in Professional Counseling at Liberty University. Author of *Reclaiming Sanity*.

Anyone recovering from trauma knows healing happens not instantly, but one day at a time. Mary DeMuth is a great companion for that journey. Drawing on her own experience of healing from sexual abuse, she takes readers through all 66 books of the Bible and helps them find wisdom, comfort, and courage in the words of God himself.

—Dr. Sandra Glahn, associate professor of Media Arts and Ministry, general editor of *Vindicating the Vixens*, and coauthor of *Sexual Intimacy in Marriage*

I have a list of books that God has used to encourage, inspire, and give me hope through my healing journey. I am adding Mary DeMuth's *Healing Every Day* to that list. Her beautiful writing and honest sharing draw readers into the truths of Scripture and close to the Lord who truly is bigger than our stories.

—Jeanette Hanscome, author of *Suddenly Single Mom*

Clients come to counseling in pain, and that's especially true in cases of abuse or severe attachment trauma. For years, I've longed for a book that could accompany clients through the difficult process of healing. That Mary DeMuth wrote it means you're getting a book from one who has walked the painful journey to health and who, by the way, happens to be a quite serious student of Scripture. I will definitely recommend this to my clients.

—Chuck Roberts, MA, LPC-S, www.life-rest-soul.com

In *Healing Every Day*, Mary once again shares her heart for those who hurt with heavy burdens and encourages them in a way that leaves them feeling like warriors. Mary is a humble leader who has been through tough times herself and takes the reader through each day, allowing them to receive validation and support through the stories of those who've gone before us in Scripture. This book is a perfect gift for when you just don't know how to speak into a tough situation.

—Emily Potter, center director, Options Pregnancy Center, Alpena, Michigan

For anyone on a journey to heal from abuse of any kind, Mary beautifully weaves biblical truths with personal experience to faithfully lead the reader to hope and healing found only in Jesus Christ. As both a survivor of sexual abuse and a mentor to others, I have no doubt this book will be a treasured resource among many for generations to come.

—Crystal Sutherland, Author of *Journey to Heal.*
Founder and president of Journey to Heal Ministries.

Healing Every Day is the devotional anyone working on healing from trauma needs. Mary writes powerfully comforting words that give readers what their hearts desperately need—the knowledge that they are not alone in how they feel and the confidence that God sees them, cares deeply about what is happening to them, and is at work in their circumstances.

—Aurora Gregory, business motivator and marketing coach, AuroraGregory.com. Author of *Get Picked.*

Healing Every Day is an ideal companion for everyone who is recovering from trauma or abuse of any kind. Mary does not shy away from the difficulties that are part of every recovery journey, but instead combines Scripture and her own journey to paint a tapestry of hope, of forgiveness, and of the tender presence of God even in the midst of terrible events. I am a survivor of a wildly abusive alcoholic home, and these pages brought me peace on a deeper level than I've known.

—Chris Morris, general editor of *Whispers in the Pews* and author of *Perfectly Abnormal*

For those of us who have endured trauma, especially those who have been retraumatized by the cold indifference or cruel indictment of triumphalist, institutionalized religion, Mary DeMuth's *Healing Every Day* is both garden of refuge and spring of refreshment.

—Noel Bouché, vision advocate, pureHOPE

To live an abundant life in Christ, we must allow Jesus into those places to bring healing. Mary's ability to identify as a survivor herself provides us with grace-filled comfort; Holy Spirit breathed nourishment and the cool, refreshing water of His presence.

—Athena Dean Holtz, founder and publisher of Redemption Press; author of *Full Circle*

This Book Belongs To:

Mary DeMuth

Healing
EVERY
DAY

HARVEST HOUSE PUBLISHERS
EUGENE, OREGON

Cover by Emily Weigel Design

Cover photo © Bukhavets Mikhail / Shutterstock

Mary E. DeMuth is represented by David Van Diest from the Van Diest Literary Agency, 34947 SE Brooks Road, Boring, OR 97009.

Healing Every Day

Copyright © 2019 Mary DeMuth
Published by Harvest House Publishers
Eugene, Oregon 97408
www.harvesthousepublishers.com

ISBN 978-0-7369-7651-0 (pbk.)
ISBN 978-0-7369-7652-7 (eBook)

Library of Congress Cataloging-in-Publication Data

Names: DeMuth, Mary E., 1967- author.
Title: Healing every day : a 90-day journey through the Bible for those who are hurting / by Mary E. DeMuth.
Description: Eugene : Harvest House Publishers, 2019.
Identifiers: LCCN 2018034451 (print) | LCCN 2018052037 (ebook) | ISBN 9780736976527 (ebook) | ISBN 9780736976510 (pbk.)
Subjects: LCSH: Healing--Biblical teaching. | Healing--Religious aspects--Christianity--Prayers and devotions.
Classification: LCC BS680.H4 (ebook) | LCC BS680.H4 D46 2019 (print) | DDC 242/.4--dc23
LC record available at https://lccn.loc.gov/2018034451

Printed in the United States of America

19 20 21 22 23 24 25 26 27 / VP-RD / 10 9 8 7 6 5 4 3 2 1

To Patrick DeMuth,
my best friend, theological mentor, career coach,
and partner in this grace-filled adventurous life.
I love you, and I'm grateful for you every day.

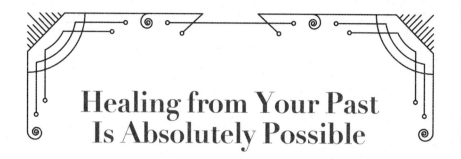

Healing from Your Past Is Absolutely Possible

I am living proof. I don't share this to brag or to put myself up as a paradigm of healing virtue. In fact, my healing journey has been full of stops and starts (majoring on the stops). I have railed at God, thrusting my fist skyward in wrath. I asked all the questions: "Why, God? If you say you love me, why didn't you prevent all that sexual abuse when I was five years old? Where were you when my home hosted scary drug parties? Why didn't you rescue me from such isolating loneliness? Why is it difficult now for me to enjoy sex because of what I went through as a child? Why does the trauma from the past—sins against me I certainly didn't invite—still affect me today? Why do I still startle easily?"

And yet, I can tell you that I have healed. Not completely. Not utterly. But enough to unearth the kind of purpose that brings me incredible joy. That's my heart for you in writing this 90-day devotional—to take you on a journey of healing through the entire counsel of Scripture toward a healthier, whole heart. You'll read at least one verse from every book of the Bible, from Genesis to Revelation, gleaning its wisdom as it pertains to your past trauma and present healing. Every entry ends with a prayer, giving you something tangible to do every day of this three-month odyssey.

Before you embark on this adventure, would you consider doing something a little risky? Find one person who loves you and ask that friend or family member to pray you through this book. Tell them your hope for healing. Share what areas of your life you're currently struggling with (Addiction? Fear? Panic? Sin? Depression? Immobilization?) and ask for them to pray that God would address these issues in your

heart. If possible, sit down with that person and pray together. Why? Because the most healing I've encountered in my journey has erupted from prayer. Perhaps your friend would be willing to read *Healing Every Day* with you through this journey. Or maybe a group of like-minded friends? Why? Because in addition to the counsel of Scripture and prayer from others, healthy community is another pathway toward the healing and wholeness you're looking for.

So, read this book. Pray through this book. And if you find your 90-day journey helpful, share this book with friends so they'll begin their own healing adventure.

Mind if I pray for you?

> *Jesus, I pray for my new friend reading this book. Would you show yourself faithful? Pursue their heart as they embark on this healing adventure. Reveal your love. Unmask the lies. Rejuvenate waning hope. Give them fresh perspective on a difficult past. I pray for a new way of seeing that past—as a gift—in light of the story you are writing in their lives. Heal broken memories. Release joy. Unfurl grace. Thank you that your love is not dependent on their perfection. Thank you that you love them even when they're messy. Thank you that you can handle any honesty they fling your way. Be near in this healing journey. Open eyes. Be tender. Radically change them from frightened to flying. I trust you to do beautiful work. Amen.*

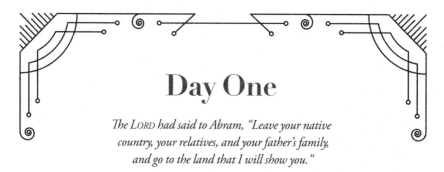

Day One

The LORD had said to Abram, "Leave your native country, your relatives, and your father's family, and go to the land that I will show you."

GENESIS 12:1

When God called Abram, he beckoned him away from everything familiar into the wild unknown. In this, he established his covenant, preparing a people for his glory and inaugurating eventual salvation through Jesus. What if Abram had said no? What if he allowed fear to crowd out the voice of God?

For those who have suffered, God often offers a similar call (although not as wide-sweeping as this specific call to Abram) to move away from the familiar to the unfamiliar. Our easygoing *known*, though full of anguish, is preferable to what is unknown—because we have no road map for living with a healthy, healed perspective. I have certainly been in that place where living under the shadow of my past is familiar. The past is like a favorite old coat—threadbare, but comfy—and the thought of having to go to a store, look for a new jacket, and pay for it leaves me overwhelmed. May as well keep the old coat.

The problem is this: The way we've coped with the past no longer works. We live fear-filled lives. We cannot seem to grow beyond pain that occurred years ago, yet still feels fresh. Instead of engaging with others, we wall off our hearts. When hard conversations arise, we shrink back, preferring silence. When you find yourself in that place, settle your heart quietly before God, listening for the echo of his call into new adventures. He is calling you away from bad coping mechanisms, beyond stuffing your past into a convenient box, further from repeating the same sins others perpetrated against you, and onward

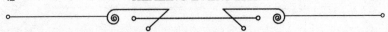

toward a brand-new life—a wide-open space full of grace and hope and trust.

Jesus asked the paralytic by the pool of Bethesda an important question: "Would you like to get well?" (John 5:6). And we have to ask ourselves the same question because we typically prefer known pain to unknown health. We would rather stay in our "native country" than venture beyond terrifying borders. Just as eventual salvation came to us because of Abram's radical obedience, you'll experience newfound emancipation if you'll simply take a step into the unknown with me in this book. Oh, how I long to see you whole, friend!

> *Jesus, I want to answer with a resounding yes when you ask me whether I want to get well. I do want health in my heart and relationships. But I'm afraid. I confess it's been easier for me to stay in the familiar pain rather than venture out toward healing. Please take my hand today and be a gentleman healer. I'm afraid, but I want to step out into an adventure of healing. Amen.*

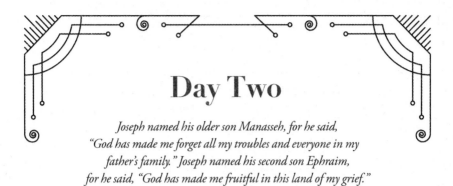

Day Two

Joseph named his older son Manasseh, for he said,
"God has made me forget all my troubles and everyone in my
father's family." Joseph named his second son Ephraim,
for he said, "God has made me fruitful in this land of my grief."

GENESIS 41:51-52

The life of Joseph is one of agonizing pain. Betrayed by his brothers, sold into slavery, lied about by Potiphar's wife, forgotten by the chief cup-bearer while in prison—he faced a slurry of relational and situational trials. You see hints of his grief as he names his sons. No longer connected to his father, mother, and brothers, alone in the world, he describes the condition of his heart with names.

Manasseh. God helped Joseph forget all his troubles and his past family. Because we know the end of Joseph's story (he ends up reuniting with his family and saving their lives, all while placed in a position of high authority by Pharaoh), we see the restoration that inevitably follows. But he names his sons when he doesn't know what will come next. And God had been gracious in helping him move on. You may relate to this. Maybe you're *in medias res,* the Latin term that simply means you're in the middle of your story and cannot see around the next bend. Pray that God would give you a Manasseh moment, an ability to move on after heartache, to let go of the past.

Ephraim. Even though Joseph had years of struggle where he certainly didn't see the fruit of his labors, he eventually did begin to see that his quiet trust in God paid off. He found joy when the final story remained sadly incomplete. But even when things began to turn around, grief remained. You see Joseph wailing, having to leave the presence of his brothers when he saw them. Perhaps you need an Ephraim prayer today, that God would bring fruitfulness to your soul

even as you grieve. Grieving is not wrong. It is not simple or quick. It is simply part of life on this earth. But even in the midst of it, God has the supernatural ability to help us thrive despite the grief. That is good news, friend.

> *Jesus, help me move on beyond the past, choosing to let go of all the pain, and find joy even today as I pray this. Thank you that grieving isn't a sin, nor should I be ashamed of it. Would you make me fruitful in the land of my grief? Would you bring me joy even when today seems less anticipatory and more gloomy? Lift my head. Lift my eyes. Lift my heart. Give me hope, the kind of hope I can trust. Amen.*

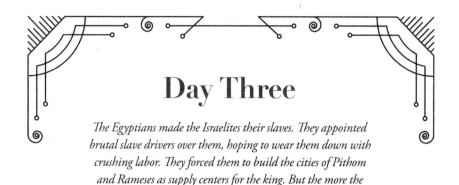

Day Three

The Egyptians made the Israelites their slaves. They appointed brutal slave drivers over them, hoping to wear them down with crushing labor. They forced them to build the cities of Pithom and Rameses as supply centers for the king. But the more the Egyptians oppressed them, the more the Israelites multiplied and spread, and the more alarmed the Egyptians became.

EXODUS 1:11-12

What a beautiful picture of perseverance and God's kindness this passage is! While the Israelites were oppressed, still they endured, even flourishing in the land of their slavery. That's my prayer for you, particularly as you revisit places where you were treated unfairly.

I've been asked how it is that I've been able to stay close to Jesus all these years. First, I wouldn't presume to say it has anything to do with me; it has everything to do with God's faithfulness. But I can honestly say that I'm now at a place where I see the past as a gift—all that heartache served as a catalyst for me to chase after Jesus, to long for him, to crave his love. My "slavery" led to my emancipation.

That's not so easy to discern, particularly if you're in the middle of your pain. I'm sure when the Israelites were gathering straw, bending under the weight of an increasingly impossible brick quota, the last thing they were thinking was that *this will lead to something better.* They could not see what God had prepared for them to walk into—literally, the dry bed of the Red Sea. They could not see milk and honey and safety.

But God still delivered them. He kept his promise. And he keeps his promise to his suffering children today. How? Through Jesus Christ. Because of his life, death, and resurrection, our past cannot taint our current joy. Empowered by the Holy Spirit, we can walk away from

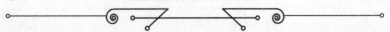

oppressive relationships. Renewed, we can experience what it means to live a life of freedom and wholeness.

So, keep walking, friend. Persevere! Your emancipation awaits. A Red Sea may loom before you, stealing your breath and any personal resolve. But you have a Savior who loves you and loves to set you free.

> *Jesus, I pray for a new perspective. I'm drowning in the sins committed against me. All of it overwhelms me, and I can't see a way out. Please help me trust you in the midst of my "slavery." Show me if there are folks I need to walk away from for the sake of my own healing. Keep me close to you as I take steps of faith away from the past. Empower me to begin to believe that I will live in freedom. Amen.*

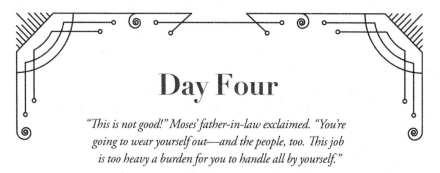

Day Four

"This is not good!" Moses' father-in-law exclaimed. "You're going to wear yourself out—and the people, too. This job is too heavy a burden for you to handle all by yourself."

EXODUS 18:17-18

The healing journey is too hard for you. You cannot do it alone, unfortunately. Just as Moses wrongly felt the sole responsibility to decide every bickering case the Israelites brought before him, we somehow think our healing is on us, and it's up to us alone. Actually, we heal best in community—which is a scary thought. When you've been wounded in negative community, God asks what seems like the impossible from us: to heal in good community.

Jethro, Moses's father-in-law, had the ability to see that Moses would burn out if he continued to handle everything on his own. He advised him to find trustworthy people to share the burden with him. And it worked. Instead of constantly hearing petty complaints, he became free to hear the important ones, while others bore the weight of the mundane disputes.

You need others. You cannot tell your story in isolation. While it can be cathartic to write it all down, you'll discover more freedom if you find trustworthy people who will bear the weight of your story alongside you. When you share your story with other believers, you're giving them the privilege of being the body of Christ to you. You're empowering them to become heroic.

Perhaps it's helpful to remember how you feel when someone comes to you for compassionate advice. It blesses you, doesn't it? You love helping others, so you see this as an opportunity to make a difference in someone else's life. Don't deny your friend that beautiful feeling by holding back and handling everything on your own.

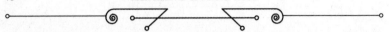

Jesus will do a significant work of healing in the quiet places of your soul. But he also will empower community to show you his love and kindness "with skin on." It's sometimes hard to experience his love, but when someone shows us that love by listening to our stories, affirming our worth, and letting us know that we're not crazy or alone, we experience him more significantly. Don't let your fear of others prevent you from this communal way of healing.

> *Jesus, I'm scared. There, I admit it. People have hurt me, broken me, raked me over the coals of this crazy, painful life. I don't want to trust them anymore. I want to retreat and lick my wounds. But I know I need others. Help me let my friends be heroic in my life. Help me share my story openly with trusted, good people. Yes, I know that I've been wounded in negative community, but I pray I'll be healed in good community. Amen.*

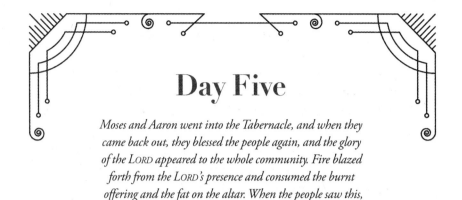

Day Five

*Moses and Aaron went into the Tabernacle, and when they
came back out, they blessed the people again, and the glory
of the LORD appeared to the whole community. Fire blazed
forth from the LORD's presence and consumed the burnt
offering and the fat on the altar. When the people saw this,
they shouted with joy and fell face down on the ground.*

LEVITICUS 9:23-24

The presence of God brings miracles. Hovering above the sphere
of the earth, it's God's presence and word that created everything
we see. And we learn in the New Testament that Jesus holds all things
together (see Colossians 1:17). The Father, the Son, and the Holy Spirit
are worthy of our affection and adoration and awe.

For those who have been hurt, it's easy to introspect. We go over
past pains in our heads until the offenses seem like cement in our memories. They loom larger than God, and we allow their narratives to have
greater sway over our decisions and livelihood.

It's time to reconsider what we worship. We are worshipping something (or a memory) when we spend time rehashing it, when we give it
space in our minds, when we dwell on it *ad infinitum*. To grow in our
healing journey, we have to reorient our minds toward the one who is
worthy of being dwelt on. God deserves the space we give him in our
minds. Instead of rehearsing and reliving our past, let's remember the
power of God. Let's worship him with everything within us, counting
his blessings, naming his attributes, and loving his nature.

When we live looking back, we can grow to a certain extent. The
negatives of the past can cause us to want to do things differently than
we experienced it. For instance, if we experienced an abusive parent,
their negative example can be a catalyst for *not* being abusive now. But

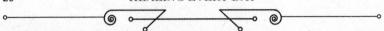

reacting to a negative only brings us so far. We grow better by looking forward and being drawn to a positive goal. When God is that powerful and positive goal, he pulls us forward, giving us the ability to overcome a dark past.

It's time to stop living tethered to the negatives of the past, and instead, look toward the bright future where the Lord already lives. Worshipping him brings you into a beautiful space. It sets you free to let go of the past and gives you the hope you need to proceed gloriously forward.

Jesus, I don't want to live in retrospect. I would rather spend my days concentrating on your goodness and love. Help me reorient my heart away from heartache and toward worshipping you. I love you, and I trust you to empower me to walk in victory today. Amen.

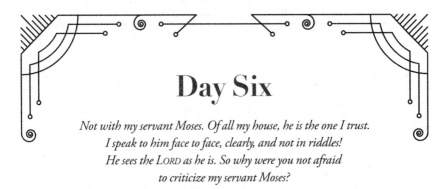

Day Six

Not with my servant Moses. Of all my house, he is the one I trust.
I speak to him face to face, clearly, and not in riddles!
He sees the LORD as he is. So why were you not afraid
to criticize my servant Moses?

NUMBERS 12:7-8

It's hard to understand that God the Father is a loving father who wants a good relationship with us. Perhaps you've experienced a painful or detrimental relationship with your earthly father. And this idea of friendship with God makes you queasy. Yet, when we look at the life of Moses, we see possible damage in his own earthly relationships. His own father was forced to abandon him, and the man who became fatherlike to him (Pharaoh) banished him from his kingdom.

And yet we see Moses in the kind of deep relationship with his heavenly Father that is open and beautiful. They talk face-to-face. God doesn't speak to him in riddles. (When we turn to the Prophets or the New Testament, we see God speaking to many in parables and riddles. He saves his clear conversations for those who want to be in a relationship with him.) Not only that, God says he trusts Moses, a mere man. How can we have that kind of relationship with God?

Of course, none of us are Moses, but because of Jesus Christ and his sacrifice on the cross, we have unfettered access to God the Father. We can now be called the friends of God because of the life, death, and resurrection of Jesus. We have the sweet opportunity to be in a close relationship with our heavenly Father.

Don't let your own broken relationship with an earthly father intimidate you from approaching the throne of grace. Your heavenly Father created you in your mother's womb. You are his image bearer. And he longs to heal you, take you from the pit that others have placed

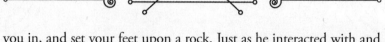

you in, and set your feet upon a rock. Just as he interacted with and loved Moses, he wants to interact with and love you. Oh, dear friend, you are loved today. Rest in that right now.

Jesus, it's easier for me to come to you because you feel more approachable to me than God the Father. Help me understand that I am loved, that the Father wants a close, intimate relationship with me. Free me from the fear of interacting with a loving heavenly Father. Oh, how I need to know I'm loved in that way. Amen.

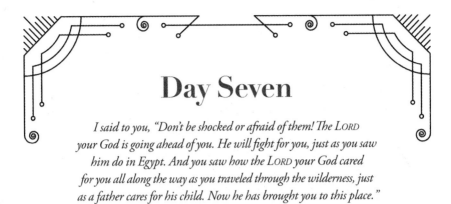

Day Seven

I said to you, "Don't be shocked or afraid of them! The LORD
your God is going ahead of you. He will fight for you, just as you saw
him do in Egypt. And you saw how the LORD your God cared
for you all along the way as you traveled through the wilderness, just
as a father cares for his child. Now he has brought you to this place."

DEUTERONOMY 1:29-31

When you face healing, the predominant emotion is often fear. To open up that Pandora's box of memories, triggers, and emotions feels like a foolhardy thing to do. Best to keep things shuttered and quiet. Except for this: Your past is still haunting you today, and you need to be free of it. Achieving that emancipation starts by taking the next step in your healing journey—trusting that God is a good, tender father who will carry you through.

In order to bravely face the rigors of the past, begin today by recounting the ways God has delivered you, just as he delivered the Israelites from slavery and peril. God traveled before them in fire and cloud, miraculously parted the Red Sea, and provided food, water, and protection from enemies bent on destroying them. Can you find a moment today to list the ways God has preserved your life? When has he been kind to you? When did he bring deliverance? How did he shepherd you toward where you are today?

You may still be in a wilderness. That's okay. We all travel through them throughout our lives. You may even have a difficult time seeing the goodness of God in the land of the living. That's okay too. Maybe your recounting of his faithfulness begins by simply praying, "God, I'm having a hard time seeing where you delivered and cared for me. Please open my eyes to what you've already done."

The truth is this: God will not leave or forsake you. Although

difficult circumstances from the past or a today-locked wilderness seem to push against that, you can still reassure yourself of the reality of his presence. He is omnipotent (all-powerful), omniscient (all-knowing), and omnipresent (everywhere). He loves to heal and deliver his children—and as a believer, you are one of those, so profoundly beloved.

Jesus, it's hard for me to look back and discern where you've been in the broken pieces of my life. Where were you when all that pain happened? Help me understand your surprising ways of deliverance today. Empower me to count the times you have been my help and provision. Open my eyes to your hand in my life. I need to know you are with me on this healing journey. Amen.

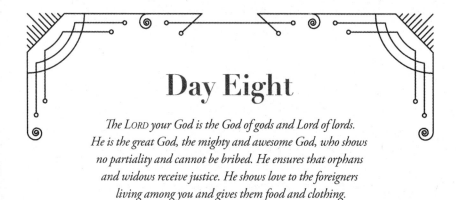

Day Eight

*The LORD your God is the God of gods and Lord of lords.
He is the great God, the mighty and awesome God, who shows
no partiality and cannot be bribed. He ensures that orphans
and widows receive justice. He shows love to the foreigners
living among you and gives them food and clothing.*

DEUTERONOMY 10:17-18

That God cannot be bribed shows his complete impartiality. He is the most capable of enacting perfect justice. And because God the Father sent the Son to the cross to pay for the sins of all of us (both the sins we committed and the sins committed against us), he is also merciful and full of grace—all things we need on this healing adventure.

This passage also reminds us just how big God is. He is bigger than perpetrators. He is bigger than violence, hatred, and indifference. He is bigger than the trauma you still face. He is bigger than triggers and nightmares and worries that keep you up at night. He is bigger than your story (he is writing it still). He is bigger than exploitation, widowhood, and orphanhood, and he is particularly attuned to the cries of the broken.

All this is good news, but it's not merely that God is big. It's that he has the biggest, most compassionate heart toward his children. He grieves when his children hurt. He is angered when they're exploited.

Because Jesus walked this earth, he has particular empathy for those who live in the margins of life. He empowered the downcast, listened to the homeless, brought forward the ones in the background of Palestine, loved the unloved, and praised the forgotten. He is that same God today, searching for the lost, finding them, and welcoming them into his kingdom.

He loves you. He is *for* you. He already knows the cries of your

heart. He sees your loneliness, struggles, and difficult relationships. He understands your wants and needs. And he knows precisely what you need in order to find healing today. That kind of Savior seems almost too good to be true, and yet he is true. He is just. He is good. And oh, how he loves you! Please settle yourself into that truth today.

> *Jesus, help me understand your immenseness. But even as I think of your justice and power, remind me that you're concerned with the minutiae of my heart. I'm struggling today, and I need to know you see me. My heart is torn apart from the past, and I long to be made whole and healthy. I give you permission today to gently lead me on the path of healing. I'm scared, but I choose to trust your heart today. Amen.*

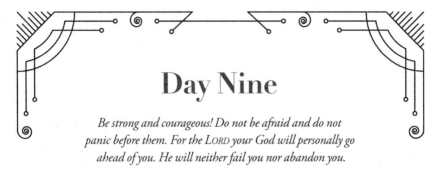

Day Nine

Be strong and courageous! Do not be afraid and do not panic before them. For the LORD your God will personally go ahead of you. He will neither fail you nor abandon you.

DEUTERONOMY 31:6

You may think you're not strong or courageous. Perhaps life has broken you down, stolen your voice, worn your heart clear out. Maybe you've given into panic of late and can't seem to steady your breath or heartbeat. Anxiety might be the hallmark of your present life.

Oh, how the Lord loves you, dear one full of anxiety and fear. He doesn't despise your pain. He doesn't chastise you for experiencing the aftereffects of loss, predation, or neglect. No, he welcomes you, open armed. He goes ahead of you. Others may have failed you terribly. Your family or friends may have abandoned you. You may have experienced betrayal at the hands of those you thought had your back, but even so, God is different. He is the one who walks before you. He prepares your way.

For many, the word *abandonment* strikes fear. It reminds us of those times in our lives when we felt utterly alone and helpless, left to fend for ourselves. Perhaps we've had to be hospitalized all alone, or maybe we suffered abuse and no other person bothered to notice the telltale signs. When we've been abandoned, we make vows to never get ourselves into those vulnerable positions again. We place fortresses around our hearts, entirely fearful of trusting another human again because fear reigns in our lives.

Because there are portions of our stories where we've felt abandoned by God, we even shift that fear of other human beings to God, pushing him away out of worry. He is our very source of light and life, but we've contented ourselves to stay far away. While it's entirely normal

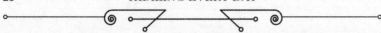

to be angry with God for perceived abandonment (and he knows your heart and feelings about this already), we will cut off the very source of healing he provides if we continue to push against him.

You may feel abandoned by God, but today's verse reminds us of solid truth: God will go ahead of you. He will not fail or abandon you. It takes a step (a leap!) of faith to believe that, but it is true. Memorize Deuteronomy 31:6; tuck it away in your heart and mind. And when you're facing another scary day, pull it out and rest your heart against it.

> *Jesus, I want to believe you will never fail or abandon*
> *me. When I look back on the holes of my life, I see pain,*
> *and I can't seem to understand your goodness. Help me*
> *orient my mind to believe your affection for me. I no*
> *longer want to be ruled by panic and anxiety. I need*
> *you. I choose you. I don't want to build a wall between*
> *us, and if I have, please gently tear it down. Amen.*

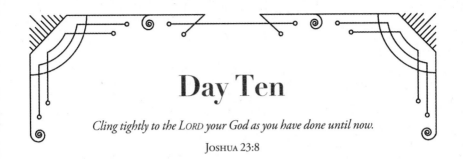

Day Ten

Cling tightly to the Lord your God as you have done until now.

JOSHUA 23:8

The Hebrew word for *cling* here is *dabaq*, which means to adhere (glue) or "to catch by pursuit."[1] In other words, we pursue God, then glue ourselves to him. Joshua had this pattern of following God his entire life, and now God is encouraging him to persevere in that same matter of pursuit. So many times we see biblical characters or people in our sphere of influence start well but finish poorly. There are many reasons for this, but often, giving up is related to losing hope. We begin to believe that our story doesn't matter. We think that how we obey or don't obey has little consequence on this life or the life to come, so we skate by, doing the minimal effort, waiting for heaven's shores in discouragement.

I believe there is more, so much more, to our lives here on earth. Simply put, your suffering is counted. It's part of your beautiful act of spiritual warfare. Even if no one else shares your pain and anguish over the past, God knows, and your faithfulness to him in the darkness matters in the spiritual realm. When you tenaciously believe God when no one's looking, you are saying to the principalities and powers out there that God is good and worth pursuing and clinging to. That shakes the heavens and the earth. It reminds the enemy of your soul, whose aim is to steal, kill, and destroy (John 10:10), that you will not be his casualty.

It is never easy to keep going, to continue to obey God in the darkness, to persevere through trials. Just ask any bicyclist who has accomplished her long-distance goals—she will tell you that it took getting on the bike every day, rain or shine, to get to that place of mastery.

Yes, you have experienced handicaps. Your life may not be going the way you've planned or anticipated. Others have been roadblocks to joy.

Some have stolen from you. But God has remained ever faithful, and his desire for you? Joy. Peace. Hope. All of which come from him. Pursue him today, friend. And when you grasp for him in the dark, don't let go until you breathe your very last breath.

Jesus, I want to remain faithful to you, despite how things worked out in the past. I seemed to have been able to persevere through those trials, but I'm weary and losing hope these days. I want to pursue you until my dying breath. I long to cling to you. Give me the energy I need, empowered by the Holy Spirit, to experience you today. Oh, how I love you. Amen.

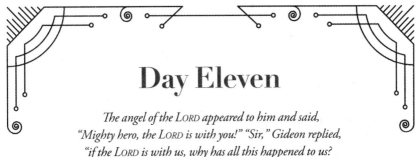

Day Eleven

*The angel of the Lord appeared to him and said,
"Mighty hero, the Lord is with you!" "Sir," Gideon replied,
"if the Lord is with us, why has all this happened to us?
And where are all the miracles our ancestors told us about?
Didn't they say, 'The Lord brought us up out of Egypt'?
But now the Lord has abandoned us and
handed us over to the Midianites."*

JUDGES 6:12-13

Have you ever felt like God has been there for you in the past, but now has left you to fend for yourself? Or maybe you hear other people's stories of God's exploits on their behalf and lament that your experience of him seems distant or nonexistent? Gideon is in this similar stage of lament. He is asking the question many of us ask: "Where are the miracles?"

When life sidelines us, and when people seem to be bent on hurting us, we may believe, like Gideon, that God has abandoned us and handed us over to toxic people.

Take note of how this interaction started, though. God calls Gideon something he likely doesn't believe about himself. He doesn't even seem to hear it or recognize what God is saying. The angel of the Lord calls Gideon a "mighty hero"—this man who was hiding out in a winepress, afraid and defeated. But God saw what would happen next. He knew that he would empower Gideon with a tiny army to defeat Israel's foes spectacularly. And that victory would have nothing to do with Gideon's amazing abilities. No, it would be all about God's capabilities.

How does this relate to you—someone desperate to heal from the past? As with Gideon, God is calling you a mighty warrior. You may feel like a mighty *worrier* instead, but that fear does not negate God's

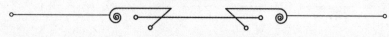

ability to work in and through you. Instead of seeing your weakness as disqualification, realize it's the ticket you need to experience the show of his power.

You are not abandoned. You are not without hope. That's what the enemy of your soul wants you to believe and internalize. The truth is this: God is with you. He will fight on your behalf. He is the mighty one. He sees *you* as a mighty warrior, despite what you see as glaring handicaps. Instead of hiding your life in fear, step out, dear one, and believe that what comes next is going to be sanctioned and empowered by your mighty God.

> *Jesus, I don't feel much like a mighty warrior today. And when I look back at my life, particularly the difficulties, I have a hard time understanding where you are. Have you abandoned me? Can I hope again? Help me trust your strength when weakness reigns in my life. I cannot heal from my past on my own. I need you today. Amen.*

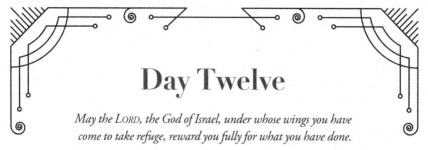

Day Twelve

May the Lord, the God of Israel, under whose wings you have
come to take refuge, reward you fully for what you have done.

RUTH 2:12

B oaz shares this with Ruth, who followed her mother-in-law, Naomi, to Israel. He praises her for her faithfulness, not only to Naomi, but also to Naomi's God. The two women are in a desperate situation and will not survive without the intervention of the Almighty.

Have you ever felt this way? That you couldn't finagle your way out of a situation? Perhaps you've had others in your care, and you felt the deep sting of fear when it came to providing for them. The weight of that feels ironlike. Where do you go when you're at the end of your capabilities? Where do you turn? As we see in today's verse, Ruth turns to God.

In the book of Ruth, God delivers both Naomi and Ruth, but not in a straightforward way—which is a huge reminder to those of us suffering and longing for help. God's answers to our prayers of "Help!" are entirely creative and surprising. We need to be careful not to prescribe to God the exact manner in which he should become our provision. So many times, we bind God to our expectations, and when he doesn't answer in the way we want him to, we automatically assume negative intent of the Almighty. God's answers differ from our expectations, which makes the adventure more adventurous, don't you think?

The beauty of Ruth's story is that it's not confined to her lifetime. She and Naomi are both delivered from poverty, yes, but Ruth's marriage to Boaz is woven into the lineage of King David, and then the King of kings, Jesus. When we're in the throes of our broken stories, we can become myopic, thinking it's all about us—when, in reality, God

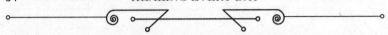

is enacting a crazy and glorious plan for the entire world, and we are simply a part of that unfolding.

> *Jesus, I don't understand your ways. Help me remember*
> *that the power of Ruth's story is not merely her deliverance,*
> *but your supernatural creation of stories beyond her story.*
> *Help me realize that your creative answers to prayer are*
> *not merely for my own healing and benefit, but that*
> *you are working for the good of the world and your ever-*
> *unfolding redemption story. Amen.*

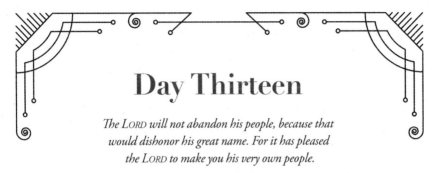

Day Thirteen

*The LORD will not abandon his people, because that
would dishonor his great name. For it has pleased
the LORD to make you his very own people.*

1 SAMUEL 12:22

As I mentioned earlier, the word *abandon* haunts many people
who have survived trauma and past pain. It connotes an utter dismissal of a person, a cynical vacating, leaving the person alone, afraid,
and longing for rescue. When we see abandoned animals on the streets
of our cities, we feel pity. We wonder who could do such a thing. But
the truth is, people abandon people in hundreds of different ways.

Some parents emotionally leave their children in the midst of their
deepest needs. Some siblings abandon each other when one cries out
for relief from a predator. The authorities (teachers, social workers,
mandatory reporters) abandon children when they simply don't want
to be bothered by the messiness of involvement. Churches abandon
victims, particularly if abuse happens within its ranks. Best friends
abandon each other via misunderstandings. Social media connections
vilify, then abandon one another at a swift rate.

We live in a world where abandonment has been normalized. Yet,
just because it's common does not mean it's easy to move past.

God built us for community, for conversation, for fellowship. He
created the first man and woman to represent the beauty of his own
dance of community in his triune nature. So when we run away from
relationships, we miss out on aspects of one another and God himself
that he desires for us to experience.

How can we begin to move toward safe community when so many
people have walked away from us? How do we trust again? We start by
memorizing today's verse. It is antithetical to God's nature to abandon

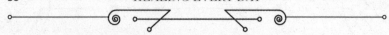

us. To do so would be to violate his character, and he cannot do that. So we can trust fully that he will never, ever walk away from us. We're not too needy, too broken, too hurt. He doesn't run from our need. He embraces us in the midst of it. In the arms of God, we can finally work through our own abandonment issues and inaugurate (slowly) new relationships that represent kindness and safety.

> *Jesus, how I need to know today that the Father, you, and the Holy Spirit will never, ever abandon me. I cannot push you away by my pain or neediness. Help me rest in the realization that you are true to your word and your nature. You simply cannot abandon your creation, and I am one of your beloved children. I'm afraid to trust others. I bear many scars of betrayal and abandonment. Please hold me close in your embrace so I can take tentative steps toward community again. Amen.*

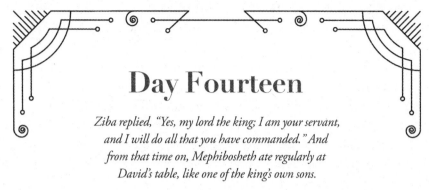

Day Fourteen

Ziba replied, "Yes, my lord the king; I am your servant, and I will do all that you have commanded." And from that time on, Mephibosheth ate regularly at David's table, like one of the king's own sons.

2 Samuel 9:11

Mephibosheth was the son of David's good friend Jonathan and Saul's grandson. He'd been crippled after his nurse dropped him when he was five years old. Though customary for new kings to extinguish the family of the predecessor, King David did not pursue or kill Mephibosheth as his nurse took him and fled. The crippled boy became a man and lived in a town named Lo-debar, which means "land of nothing."

David searched for survivors of Saul's family, then was told about Mephibosheth and sent for him. He insisted the crippled man eat at the king's table and be financially restored. What a beautiful picture of redemption! From living in the "land of nothing" to dining at the king's table.

This is the picture of healing Jesus created for us. Like Mephibosheth, we did nothing to make ourselves crippled—someone else caused it. Nor could we choose our heritage (like Mephibosheth's being Saul's grandson). In light of all this, Mephibosheth should have lived in terrified exile in those days, but instead, David searched the known world for this man. He validated him, dignified him, then restored him to significance.

Like the good shepherd who pursues the one, leaving the ninety-nine, Jesus pursued us, even when we chose to go astray, living in the land of nothing. He rewrote our stories from crippled outcasts to

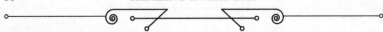

beloved friends. He welcomed us at his table, restoring us to life and dignity again.

But what if Mephibosheth had protested? What if he'd fought to stay in Lo-debar? What if he ran in fear from the one who set him free? He would have remained broken, unfulfilled, and lonely. God's beckoning to you today is that of David: "Come dine at my table. Don't be afraid. I will protect and restore you."

Like Mephibosheth, it's time to say yes to your redeemer. I know it's hard to understand or even receive outlandish love like that, but you'll never experience the riches and joys of the king's table if you don't accept his beckoning invitation.

> *Jesus, sometimes I feel like Mephibosheth. Someone else*
> *has harmed me, crippled my heart, and I'm sitting in the*
> *land of nothing, feeling abandoned and isolated. But*
> *no more. Today, I choose to listen to your invitation. I'm*
> *afraid to accept it, but I want to do it. Give me the "want*
> *to" to receive from you, to be restored to dignity again.*
> *Oh, how I want to eat at your table today. Amen.*

Day Fifteen

*Tamar tore her robe and put ashes on her head. And
then, with her face in her hands, she went away crying.*

2 SAMUEL 13:19

The Bible doesn't shy away from truth. It doesn't sugarcoat violation. Here we see Tamar, a rape victim, grieve profoundly after her half brother Amnon assaulted her, then treated her like refuse. In her culture, when Amnon forcibly stole her virginity, he stole her life and livelihood. A nonvirgin was considered damaged and most likely would not be married. She would be financially dependent on her family the rest of her life, and she would live in utter shame.

Which is why we see her grieving here. That kind of violation represents death to her, so in the same fashion someone would grieve the loss of a loved one, she throws ashes on her head and weeps.

She demonstrates something profound for all of us who have suffered differing levels of violation. We need to grieve. Sometimes insincere people will ask me, "Why can't you just get over the past? The rapes happened so long ago. Let it go!"

To them, I ask, "Have you ever lost a loved one?"

Most say, "Yes."

"Then how long did it take to 'get over' that loss?" If the person is honest, they'll admit that the grief lasted a long time, and that you never really "get over" losing someone. Sadness lessens and improves, but the loss remains. That's the way it is for victims of assault, betrayal, and abandonment. In order to move toward health, we must start with grief.

Unlike Tamar, many of us would rather pretend the violation never happened. If we can trick ourselves into believing it didn't occur, we can move on quickly with our lives. The problem is, when we stuff

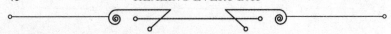

down emotions and memories, harmful actions erupt. We only heal in relation to our admission of initial grief, and that process of grieving parallels God's process of healing for us. If you haven't yet grieved, find a safe person and let your story out. It's your first step toward freedom.

> *Jesus, I would rather shut down all this, forgetting the past. Why dredge it up? Didn't you make all things new? But I'm tired of my grief popping out through damaging actions on my part. Teach me to be like Tamar and grieve, to let out this pain I've stuffed inside for so long. I'm terrified, Jesus. Worried that if I open the lid, all sorts of grief will pour out like a vat of snakes. Help me. Give me strength. Would you please grieve alongside me? Amen.*

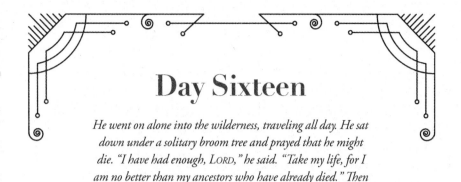

Day Sixteen

He went on alone into the wilderness, traveling all day. He sat down under a solitary broom tree and prayed that he might die. "I have had enough, LORD," he said. "Take my life, for I am no better than my ancestors who have already died." Then he lay down and slept under the broom tree. But as he was sleeping, an angel touched him and told him, "Get up and eat!"

1 KINGS 19:4-5

Elijah seems to have suffered from the depression that comes after victory. He'd called fire from heaven and watched as God demonstrated his supremacy. In the next breath, we see Jezebel, wife of King Ahab, threaten his life. So Elijah fled, and we find him here, sitting under a broom tree and begging for death.

His prayer is instructive for anyone who has walked through trauma. He is honest. He tells the almighty God, who just demonstrated amazing power on his behalf, that he's had enough. Have you ever prayed something similar to Elijah's prayer? (Elijah had more "famous" prayers about drought and rain, but this one never seems to be highlighted!)

Have you longed to be set free from your current sadness, preferring death over life? So did Elijah. He was known as a mighty prophet, and yet he hurt this way. This is great encouragement! Your weariness and depressive burdens do not mean that you're unloved by God, or that he cannot use you. Unfortunately, in our churches today, we're often told to claim victory or "get over it already" when we're hurting as Elijah did. We somehow believe we're at fault or we don't have enough faith to overcome our mood. No, we are simply normal human beings responding to trauma.

Note God's response. He didn't chastise Elijah for his honesty. He didn't send more fire from heaven to destroy a "faithless" prophet. He

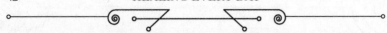

didn't shake his head, disappointed. No, he sent a messenger to rouse him. He supplied food for Elijah, who was most likely exhausted, hungry, and deeply discouraged. He met the needs of the prophet as a loving father. That is how our God sees you, dear friend. He allows your rants. He shoulders your pain. And he longs to provide for you when life feels the bleakest. Take heart.

> *Jesus, I admit there have been times in my life where death felt like the perfect escape from my ongoing pain. I have walked the road of discouragement. I have faced many painful trials. I have lost relationships dear to me. I have acquired enemies bent on hurting me. All that exhausts me, to be honest. I need to know you're watching over me. Please provide what my heart needs today. Amen.*

Day Seventeen

Hezekiah trusted in the LORD, the God of Israel. There was no one like him among all the kings of Judah, either before or after his time. He remained faithful to the LORD in everything, and he carefully obeyed all the commands the LORD had given Moses.

2 KINGS 18:5-6

I t's not easy trusting in a God you cannot see. It's hard enough trusting people you can see, especially those who hurt you or walk away from you when you're in the midst of pain. But to trust God? Difficult. Hezekiah mastered this by remaining faithful to God no matter what. To be faithful, the text says, is to obey the commands of God.

When we look to the New Testament and see Jesus, we watch him distill the Ten Commandments into two: love God; love others (see Matthew 22:37-40). If we want to be faithful, trusting followers, we do those two things.

How do we love God when life hurts us so much? It's easier to blame God, to point the finger his way. After all, he is sovereign over the whole world. He is the great I Am—the God of the present tense—living, moving, and breathing over this world. Why couldn't he stop all that bad stuff from happening to us? Why did he allow so much suffering in our lives? In the world?

Of course, these are ancient questions, not easily answered. But the core is this: God loves us and gives us all autonomy over our choices. And some choices we make hurt others—or we are hurt by others' choices. We also live in a fallen world. Things aren't as they should be, so we see earthquakes and famine and tsunamis swallow up this current world. We live in the tension of autonomy and fallenness. And yet, God is good. To love him is to work toward believing that, this side of heaven.

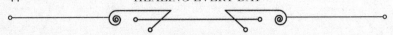

To love others means to dignify them as image bearers (*imago dei*) of God. This extends even to those human beings who hurt us. This doesn't mean we are unwise, choosing to be abused by people. But it does inform our prayers for them. We fight to see God in the midst of our foes, remembering that God loves them as much as he loves us.

These are not easy ways to obey—to trust that God is good or to see his goodness in an enemy—but both will profoundly assist in your healing journey.

> *Jesus, help me understand your goodness and trust your heart as Hezekiah did. I want to be faithful to you, even as I question why bad things happen to folks or why it's so hard to love those who hurt me. Give me wisdom, please, as to how to pray for those who have wronged me. I need you in this journey. Amen.*

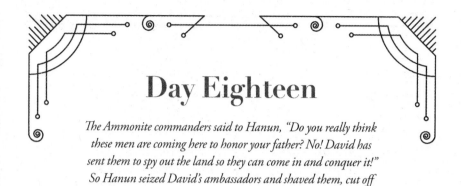

Day Eighteen

*The Ammonite commanders said to Hanun, "Do you really think
these men are coming here to honor your father? No! David has
sent them to spy out the land so they can come in and conquer it!"
So Hanun seized David's ambassadors and shaved them, cut off
their robes at the buttocks, and sent them back to David in shame.*

1 CHRONICLES 19:3-4

Hanun assumed negative intent on David's part. He believed his
Ammonite commanders over the reputation of the king of Israel.
Instead of waiting and seeking to find out David's intentions (which
were good—David wanted to honor Hanun and give genuine condo-
lences over the loss of his father), he hotheadedly jumped to conclu-
sions with disastrous consequences.

Hanun shamed and humiliated David's envoys. Beardless and
bare-legged, the men returned to their king, heads bowed. The result?
War and the destruction of Hanun's people.

We can learn from Hanun's negative example. Most likely grieving and in a vulnerable spot, Hanun was in a weakened position for
thinking cautiously. And when we are in difficult circumstances and
our emotions are threadbare, we, too, can make awful decisions. So
when you're grieving, pay careful attention to the way you treat people. If you catch yourself jumping to a conclusion, instead of reacting
immediately, slow yourself down. Take care of your heart. Ask others
to pray. This will help prevent disaster and rash actions. Most humil-
iation is also prevented, both for us and those we hurt, when we ask
open-ended questions.

Are you weak today? Weary from grief? Tired of hurting? Realize,
then, that you're in a vulnerable place. Don't make big decisions. Take
a step back and care for yourself. Rest. Do something rejuvenating. Get

help. Seek counsel. Don't compound today's grief by making a rash decision—ensuring you'll create even more grief tomorrow. Instead, slow down.

It's helpful when you're myopic about today's sadness to think about blessing your future self. It's certainly not helpful if today's self assumes negative things of others and hurts them in retaliation. Your future self will have to navigate the hurt of another, apologize, and backtrack. So bless yourself today and rest.

Jesus, I don't want to be mired in my sadness so much that I can't see other people's hearts correctly. I don't want to live in this world with grief-colored glasses forever. Would you show me ways to rest and rejuvenate today? I want to bless my future self with good, healthy decisions. Amen.

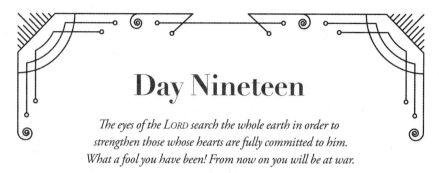

Day Nineteen

The eyes of the LORD search the whole earth in order to strengthen those whose hearts are fully committed to him. What a fool you have been! From now on you will be at war.

2 CHRONICLES 16:9

H anani the seer says these words to Asa, the king of Judah, who had started well by tearing down pagan altars and deposing his grandmother, who worshipped Asherah, a foreign goddess. He sought God through most of his reign, particularly when faced with war. But later, when Baasha, king of Israel, barricaded Judah, Asa panicked, using the temple treasury to bribe a pagan nation to protect him from invasion.

When Hanani speaks of a heart fully committed to God, he uses the Hebrew terminology *lebab shalem,* which means "wholehearted devotion." His criticism is implied in these verses: God seeks those whose hearts are bent toward him; he wants those who seek him with wholehearted devotion. Now that Asa has bent his heart away from God, serving both a pagan nation and his God, he will experience war.

We can learn much from King Asa as wounded folks on a difficult healing journey. Often, we start well. We pursue God wholeheartedly. We seek wholeness and healing. We ask for prayer. We seek wise counsel and attend support groups and counseling. But then we grow weary. The journey toward health is long, with many pitfalls. We may even suffer a major setback as Asa did (in his case, an impending invasion). And when that happens, the temptation will arise to fall back into old patterns of behavior, to do things the way the world has always done them. It may seem like the easiest, most logical thing to do, but if our reaction does not involve God or seeking him for help, we will inevitably shortchange our healing journey.

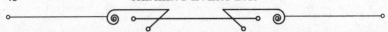

Healing is hard. It is brave. And it takes wholehearted devotion—
not to formulas or systems, but to the one who created you. While
there is warning in Hanani's words, there is also a beautiful promise.
If we don't give up, if we continue to press in and seek God, we will
find our weary hearts strengthened. We will find strong support. We
will experience the nearness and provision of God in ways we never
could if we chose instead to trust our own wits. So stay with the journey, friend. Keep seeking God with your whole heart and await his
powerful strength.

> *Jesus, I know I've been fickle. There've been times I've*
> *chased after worldly solutions. I've also seen difficult*
> *roadblocks, and instead of running to you, I run to man-*
> *made pathways. Help me understand what it means to*
> *have a fully devoted heart. Help me bend my heart toward*
> *yours today, trusting that you're good. I'm weary, and I*
> *need your strength in this arduous healing journey. Amen.*

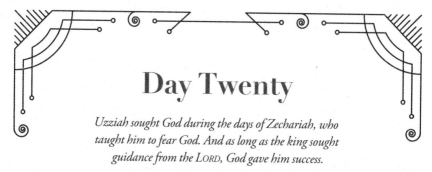

Day Twenty

Uzziah sought God during the days of Zechariah, who
taught him to fear God. And as long as the king sought
guidance from the LORD, God gave him success.

2 CHRONICLES 26:5

Like King Asa, King Uzziah started his reign well. He equipped his army, created farms, and built towns. He not only sought after God, but he also asked for guidance. As he did this, God blessed him. But notice the phrase in the middle of today's verse: "Zechariah...taught him to fear God." Uzziah learned the art of seeking God through the prophet Zechariah.

Ruling a nation is impossible work. Knowing the nature of the healing journey, I can attest that seeking after wholeness often seems similar in scope. And the truth is, we all need wise counselors to help us on this journey.

In short, we need a Zechariah or two. Healing seldom comes in isolation. Left to ourselves, we fester. Our thoughts turn wild, and we tend to believe waves upon waves of lies. In fact, those lies sound awfully similar to our own voice. If we isolate ourselves and never share what we hear in our head, we'll never truly be set free. Those lies will mutate and grow unchecked if they never see the light of day.

Sharing your story with a Zechariah is a necessary first step in your healing journey. When you bravely recount what happened to you, you let out the power of that story, much like letting the air out of a beach ball that you've tried in vain to submerge. When it's inflated, it looms large and is frustratingly difficult to keep beneath the waves. But when you "deflate" your story by sharing it, it loses its power, and you can rightly put it to rest.

What happens when you share your story? You begin to realize that

you're normal, that all people suffer, and that many folks have believed the same lies as you have. You'll understand, finally, that you are not alone. You'll have another person willing to shoulder the weight of your story. And when you bring what has felt like darkness into the light, you'll begin to experience freedom in ways you never could when you kept it all in. Find a Zechariah today—a safe and trusted person who can listen, bear your story, and empower you to thrive.

Jesus, would you send me a Zechariah? I'm not even sure whom that might be. Sometimes I've chosen unsafe people to help me bear my story, but today I need someone who is wise and kind. I know I can't do this healing journey by myself, but I am scared to open up my heart again. Give me the bravery I need to entrust my story to someone else and uncover the lies I've believed about myself. Amen.

Day Twenty-One

Now we have been given a brief moment of grace, for the LORD
our God has allowed a few of us to survive as a remnant. He has given
us security in this holy place. Our God has brightened our eyes and
granted us some relief from our slavery. For we were slaves, but
in his unfailing love our God did not abandon us in our slavery.
Instead, he caused the kings of Persia to treat us favorably.
He revived us so we could rebuild the Temple of our God and repair
its ruins. He has given us a protective wall in Judah and Jerusalem.

EZRA 9:8-9

What a beautiful paragraph describing God's intersection with the lives of his people! This was written after the Israelites were exiled to Babylon and are now returning to Jerusalem as a remnant. They'd experienced slavery, isolation, and banishment from their homeland. But God still poured himself into them in the midst of their exile.

Our testimonies often feel like exile stories. When you're exiled, it's against your will. Foreign powers have taken you away from what is good and right. They invade your home and take away your will. They force you to work. Many of us experienced similar circumstances in our childhoods. Through no fault of our own, we were harmed, exiled from what should have been, and suffered at the hand of cruel oppressors. Or maybe we were recently in the midst of a relationship that stole our voice or demeaned our character. We didn't invite the abuse, but it happened nonetheless.

Even so, God was in the midst of it. Because if you catapult yourself through Scripture into the New Testament, you'll see Jesus getting messy in humanity's story. We were enslaved to sin, broken by the world, and in dire need of rescue. He was the perfect emancipator—living a perfect life, becoming the once-for-all sacrifice on the cross,

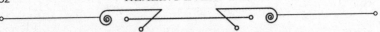

rising to life again, and defeating death forever. When he left this earth, he sent believers the Holy Spirit—a wonderful counselor who is with us always.

No matter what you have experienced or what you will experience in the days to come, God will be with you. He lives within you. He will grant you relief from your current and past situations. He will be your security. He provides unfailing love and a protective wall around your heart. Don't lose heart, dear friend. He is with you.

> *Jesus, thank you for this example in Scripture of your presence in the midst of painful circumstances. Thank you that you provide your Spirit to live within me today, giving me hope and the power to live with joy—even if people are harming me. Set me free to sing in the midst of my situation. And provide a new perspective as I sift through my past. Amen.*

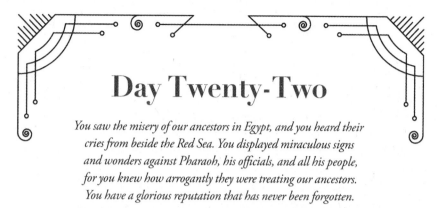

Day Twenty-Two

You saw the misery of our ancestors in Egypt, and you heard their cries from beside the Red Sea. You displayed miraculous signs and wonders against Pharaoh, his officials, and all his people, for you knew how arrogantly they were treating our ancestors. You have a glorious reputation that has never been forgotten.

NEHEMIAH 9:9-10

Sometimes in the midst of grief and pain, it's hard to remember that God has "a glorious reputation that has never been forgotten." When life slams into our resolve, we tend to become nearsighted, only able to see what is dark beyond us. We forget all the myriad feats of deliverance God has already inaugurated in our lives.

These verses in Nehemiah remind us of God's *hesed* (his unfailing covenantal love) toward his people, the nation of Israel. These words are written after many trials had invaded their lives. Licking their wounds, they've returned from exile to a Jerusalem in ruins, which Nehemiah has been tasked to rebuild. Devastation is everywhere they turn. So the leaders of the people remind them of God's faithfulness in the form of a prayer.

You can do this same faith-filled act. You always have the opportunity to express to God what he has done in your life. Instead of recounting your stress (which is an entirely normal thing to do in prayer), this time start by listing God's kindnesses toward you. How has he delivered you from misery? When has he responded to your cries for help? How has he displayed his power in your life over the past few years? When has he shown you that he sees you? Knowing the faithfulness of God, I believe you could take hours reminding him of his amazing kindness toward you. You might even get lost in his goodness while you concentrate on his reputation.

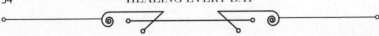

When I am overwhelmed, and the circumstances around me seem dire and thick, I'm learning the power of speaking back to God all he has done for me. In that attitude of thankfulness, I find my problems become smaller and my view of God is enlarged. I pray that same realization for you today.

Jesus, you have done so much for me. You have helped me escape from slavery and pain. You have empowered me to move beyond the past. You have shown me time and time again that you are faithful even when I'm faithless. I choose today to think about your goodness and your amazing reputation for delivering me. I want to remember again that you are big, and, compared to you, my problems are small. Amen.

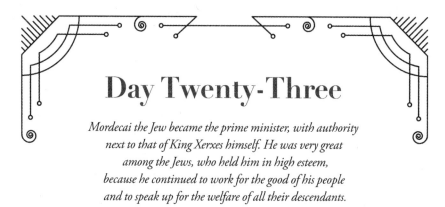

Day Twenty-Three

*Mordecai the Jew became the prime minister, with authority
next to that of King Xerxes himself. He was very great
among the Jews, who held him in high esteem,
because he continued to work for the good of his people
and to speak up for the welfare of all their descendants.*

ESTHER 10:3

One of the most surprising things I've encountered in my healing journey is the joy that comes from helping other people.
Whereas I didn't have a hero to rescue me when I was younger (and
oh, how I longed for one), I now have the privilege of being "heroic"
in other people's lives: bearing their burdens, praying for healing, and
writing books that help people find freedom. My heart nearly bursts
with the joy of seeing how my past pain has been redeemed, so much
so that I've become an agent of healing for others.

Mordecai also suffered, was delivered, then responded by living a
life of integrity and service. He worked for the sake of others, carrying
burdens and seeking the welfare of those in his care. His pattern can
be yours as well: Be hurt; be healed; become a healer.

But what if you feel like you're still stuck in the mire? What if life
feels way too dark, and your problems are far too big? What if the
thought of bearing someone else's story brings you fear? Remember,
there are seasons in all our lives. Seasons of healing. Seasons of rest. Seasons of ministry. Seasons of impact. You may be in a season of healing
and rest. And that's okay. Mordecai lived through several seasons that
must've felt a lot like trauma and foreboding. He didn't always have
the wherewithal or the position to help others. His ending of the story,
that of a life of helpfulness, is simply that: the ending. You may be in
the middle of your story, awaiting deliverance.

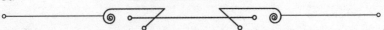

Even so, know this: There may come a time when all that misery translates into some sort of ministry, where you'll taste the fruit of your suffering. And even if not, on the other side, where God rights the wrongs and completes our stories, we will know the whys of our pain. In the meantime, in that space between the now and the not yet, keep pursuing healing and stay alert to the small ways God may empower you to help a fellow struggler.

Jesus, I pray you would help me discern what season I'm in. Am I in the midst of being delivered? Am I called to persevere through this trial? Am I in a place of being heroic for the sake of others? No matter where I find myself today, help me find joy in this moment, not over-lamenting the past nor over-glamorizing the future. Hold me today, I pray. Amen.

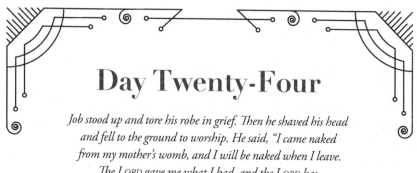

Day Twenty-Four

*Job stood up and tore his robe in grief. Then he shaved his head
and fell to the ground to worship. He said, "I came naked
from my mother's womb, and I will be naked when I leave.
The LORD gave me what I had, and the LORD has
taken it away. Praise the name of the LORD!"
In all of this, Job did not sin by blaming God.*

JOB 1:20-22

Job is the patron saint of the hurting, and here he demonstrates why. Through no fault of his own, he lost everything—most of his family, his business, many of his relationships, his health. And still he utters this faith-filled message—that all things come through the hand of God, both in giving and taking. He will choose to praise God no matter what comes his way.

But take note of how this passage starts. He tore his robe. He shaved his head. Then he worshipped. His worship commenced through grieving. Just as we learned from Tamar's response to her rape (see 2 Samuel 13), we see that grief (and allowing it) comes before healing.

In this present church era, the tendency we've seen is to limit grief. People are simply not comfortable with it, so they minimize it in themselves and others. They've forgotten that true life change comes in the midst of grief, and that growth often only comes in the midst of suffering. We run away from pain and suffering, hoping to protect ourselves from further harm, but in doing so, we shortchange our growth.

What Job teaches us is this: It's acceptable as a child of God to grieve. It's good to be honest. God is not shocked by our authenticity when we face various trials. In fact, he understands and welcomes our hearts.

This "praise the name of the Lord," though is not the end of Job's story. He spends the entire book wrestling, questioning, and being

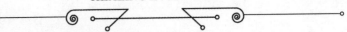

absolutely human. He began the journey hearing about God, but ended it by seeing God (see Job 42:5). He had to work through his grief, express his emotions, and share his anger with God before he began to experience God on a deeper level. So remember that it's okay to grieve—it's the gateway toward intimacy with God.

Jesus, thank you that biblical characters are three-dimensional; they honestly grieved. Thank you that you didn't despise Job for his authenticity. Thank you that you do such incredible work through those who suffer. I want to welcome that growth. I want to experience you in deeper ways. Help me share all of me with you—including my fears and frustrations—so I can experience more of you. Amen.

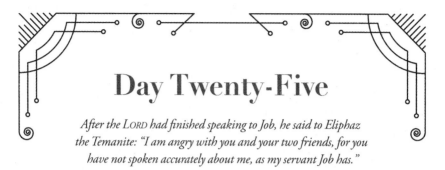

Day Twenty-Five

After the LORD had finished speaking to Job, he said to Eliphaz the Temanite: "I am angry with you and your two friends, for you have not spoken accurately about me, as my servant Job has."

JOB 42:7

J ob's friends started off well. When they saw his pain and grief, they simply approached him, sat alongside him, and said nothing. But then they opened their mouths, and all sorts of platitudes, blame, and clichés emitted from smug hearts. They told him, basically, that he deserved all his heartache, that he had harbored massive sin in his heart, and that evil people are always punished, while godly people are always blessed.

Of course, we know in a fallen world that life is never that simple. Good people walk through trials. Folks bent on evil seem to get away with it. You may even have experienced both scenarios. Maybe you're in the middle of a trial through no fault of your own. Perhaps someone who has deeply wounded you continues to hurt people, seemingly undeterred. The reality is, this world is tragically broken.

We do know the end of the story, thankfully. We can persevere because we know that when the new heavens and the new earth come, all will be made right. And we can learn to offer grace to people in our lives who try to slap a cliché bandage on our broken hearts. Sometimes people are at a loss for words and opt for insensitivity.

There are times, however, when our friends are relentless in their judgments or unswerving in their "helpful" advice. In times like those, we can learn from Job. He did offer grace, yes, but he also pushed back. He reminded his friends that evil people sometimes get away with their schemes, and sometimes folks who do the "right things" suffer under

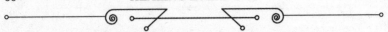

tyranny. He didn't back down. And while God highlighted Job's igno-
rance as a human being, he reserved his anger for Job's friends.

We can learn to not only push back by speaking the truth in love,
but we can also see the response of Job's friends as a cautionary tale for
the times when we walk alongside a friend who is on a healing journey. Instead of judgment and platitudes, we can simply sit and be silent.
Our gift of listening and presence will deeply impact them.

> *Jesus, I pray you would help me be the kind of friend*
> *I needed when things were dark in my life. Instead of*
> *offering up clichés and snap judgments, empower me*
> *to sit with a friend, to be present. Thank you that you*
> *didn't condemn Job for pushing back. Please give me*
> *discernment today so I can do the same in one of my*
> *current relationships. Amen.*

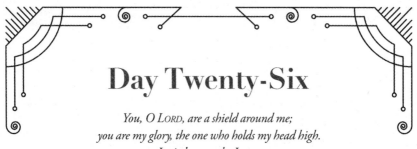

Day Twenty-Six

You, O LORD, are a shield around me;
you are my glory, the one who holds my head high.
I cried out to the LORD,
and he answered me from his holy mountain.
I lay down and slept,
yet I woke up in safety,
for the LORD was watching over me.
I am not afraid of ten thousand enemies
who surround me on every side.

PSALM 3:3-6

When life borders on chaos and the voices in your head are louder than your faith, it's always a smart practice to retreat into the reading of Scripture. And this passage is a good one to find solace in. What beautiful truths it espouses: God is our shield; he lifts our heads; he answers; he watches over us. Like a good parent who loves and protects their children, our Father in heaven has these same traits when he considers us.

Remember, though, that this was written in a snapshot of the psalmist's life. He no doubt did endure trials, sleepless nights, and predation. God is a sure refuge, but that doesn't mean we won't ever experience stress or fear or trials. Which is why, sometimes, verses like these can trip us up. We read them as truths for all time. God will *always* keep me safe. He will *always* shield me from harm. And when he doesn't, we wonder if he is good, or if he really is the powerful God he says he is. Or maybe we think, *He takes care of others, but he doesn't choose to take care of me.*

Based on our story of past abuse, it's easy to slip into this kind of

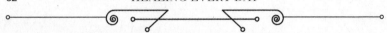

thinking. Why didn't God rescue us from those too strong? Why didn't he seem to answer our prayers? Why did he appear to stand aloof?

These are difficult questions, but they are valid ones. They are worth working through and wrestling with the Almighty about. Of course, we understand that we live in a sin-scarred world. We know that God doesn't violate the free will of those bent on evil. But he also has a grand redemptive plan that takes into account every predatory act. He redeems what was stolen from us and creates beauty from chaos. And on the other side, all will be made right. That may be frustrating in this moment, but it is assurance nonetheless. In the in-between time where we live on this earth and long for heaven, we can be assured that God will watch over us, hear us, and respond to the children he deeply loves—in his sometimes-paradoxical timing.

Jesus, I pray you'd help me work through verses like this that recount your goodness, even when I'm wrestling with the bad things that have happened to me. Give me your perspective on my suffering. Help me continue to reach out to you as I figure this out. Thank you that all will be made right someday. Amen.

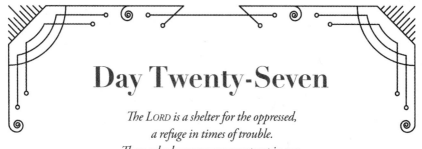

Day Twenty-Seven

The LORD is a shelter for the oppressed,
a refuge in times of trouble.
Those who know your name trust in you,
for you, O LORD, do not abandon those who search for you.

PSALM 9:9-10

Because God made the entirety of creation, including every human being on the planet, he deeply loves each one of us. He is bothered when one of his little ones suffers. He is particularly close to those who are marginalized and broken. You see his affection in Scripture when he commands the Israelites to take care of the foreigner, orphan, and widow. You see this kindness in action as Jesus goes out of his way in the Gospels to find people who are overlooked and seemingly unwanted.

This is the God you serve. This is the God who cares about what disturbs your heart, who seeks after you when you are hurting. He will not abandon you. He will bend his ear toward your cries. He will provide a refuge as you seek healing. He will shelter you when others threaten or verbally abuse you. He does his best work in the secret place of your soul, where you can retreat safely.

That's the beauty of the Christian walk—God is most easily found when we are at our most broken. Many times in Scripture, we see God aloof from the proud and all-sufficient, but he knows the broken intimately. When we are weak, we realize our ardent need for him. When we are broken, we realize we cannot live life on our own terms. When we are beaten down, we understand that we cannot succeed at life on our own, in our own strength. No, we need a Savior. We need Jesus.

Our broken hearts are catalysts to us seeking heart-healing in him. Our shelterless life causes us to find shelter in him. When we lack refuge, we long for his refuge, so we approach him. When all is well, we

often try to run our lives in our own strength, not acknowledging our need for God. But when we realize we cannot live our lives without him, we seek him and find him. We experience his sheltering refuge in the form of his presence. Personal pain becomes the avenue for us to experience the nearness of God. What a profound truth!

> *Jesus, I pray you'd help me shift my perspective today from being upset about my predicament to becoming anticipatory about discovering your strength. Thank you that you don't despise my weakness, but welcome it. Thank you that my pain becomes a deeper pathway of knowing you and experiencing your deliverance and presence. Thank you, Jesus. Amen.*

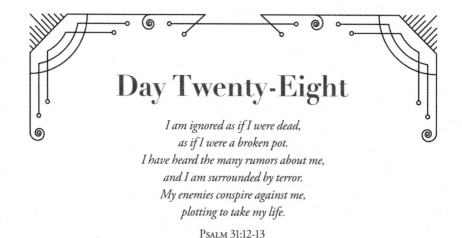

Day Twenty-Eight

I am ignored as if I were dead,
as if I were a broken pot.
I have heard the many rumors about me,
and I am surrounded by terror.
My enemies conspire against me,
plotting to take my life.

PSALM 31:12-13

Ever feel like a broken pot, shattered beyond recognition? Have you experienced the pain of being ignored? Have you endured the rumor mill? Do you ever face terror or anxiety when you walk through your days? Even though it seems strange to call someone an enemy, the truth is, we all know folks at one time or another who act enemy-like. If you've ever felt these sorrows, the good news is this: You are not alone. Others have been in dark circumstances as well, and we are blessed to read their recorded words in the Psalms.

As you continue reading Psalm 31, you'll see that God beautifully shows up. He brings relief in the midst of dire circumstances. What's telling is that he allows those circumstances in the first place. As we grow in our knowledge of him, we begin to understand the powerful truth that we grow best in adversity. Jesus tells us in the Gospels that we will have trouble in this world (see John 16:33); it is a known fact. But he also reminds us that he will be with us in the midst of it until the end of the age (see Matthew 28:20).

The important thing we learn is that even though circumstances don't always turn in our favor, and we sometimes fight battles on all fronts (in the psalmist's case, he faces isolation, brokenness, slander, fear, and the threat of harm), God will be with us. He loves to hold us through these terribly painful ordeals.

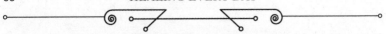

Our tendency, though, is to blame God for not rescuing us swiftly enough. Instead of leaning into the pain and seeking his paradoxical strength, we harden our hearts, then push him away, deciding prematurely that he is the cause of all our pain, or that he could have intervened, but callously chose not to. This is a normal response to unremitting stress, but in the long run, it will poison the relationship with God we so desperately need.

We must come to the point where we, like Peter, realize we have nowhere else to turn for help. He said, "Lord, to whom would we go? You have the words that give eternal life" (John 6:68). Instead of spinning our wheels and plotting against the Almighty, we are better off when we surrender and seek his help, making peace with his sometimes-frustrating plans for us.

Jesus, I'm grateful to know I'm not alone in the way I've been treated. Throughout all of history, people have been hurting people. But I'm so tired. I'm weary of the abuse, the slander, the unrelenting stress. I don't want to blame you in the midst of my struggle, but it's hard. Would you teach me what you want me to learn during this difficult season? And would you please soften my heart toward you? Only you have the words of eternal life, and I desperately need them today. Amen.

Day Twenty-Nine

O God, listen to my cry!
Hear my prayer!
From the ends of the earth,
I cry to you for help
when my heart is overwhelmed.
Lead me to the towering rock of safety,
for you are my safe refuge,
a fortress where my enemies cannot reach me.
Let me live forever in your sanctuary,
safe beneath the shelter of your wings!

PSALM 61:1-4

When I teach writing to students, I tell them that they're limited to one exclamation point per book. It's better to show excitement rather than convey it through a punctuation mark. But the translators of Psalm 61 have taken the liberty here to add three exclamation points because the text is full of desperation and need.

Isn't that true of us? When we're hurting, and we text our friends about that pain, we add lots of exclamation points to convey the seriousness of our brokenness. Here, the psalmist is desperate for God. He has cried. He has prayed—seemingly in every obscure location.

He offers us hiking metaphors: a "towering rock of safety," a refuge. Then he shifts to military might, calling God a fortress. When words appear to fail him, he moves to the spiritual metaphor of a sanctuary, then finally ends up in nature again, showing God as a mighty bird who shelters us under his wings.

What beautiful news! God is so many forms of protection that our words fail us when we try to describe him. Which shows just how limited human language can be when we try to depict God and his

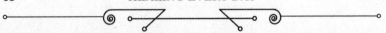

attributes. Later, in the New Testament, we see that the Holy Spirit intercedes for our desperate situations without words: "The Holy Spirit helps us in our weakness. For example, we don't know what God wants us to pray for. But the Holy Spirit prays for us with groanings that cannot be expressed in words" (Romans 8:26).

All this to say, God understands your exclamation-point prayers. He knows you are limited in fully describing your heart. He himself is impossible to describe adequately. But despite all that, the truth remains: He will protect, shelter, and provide for you in his sanctuary. He is a good God who knows your needs.

> *Jesus, I don't have words to describe how I'm feeling at any given time. I have to rely on the Holy Spirit to intercede for me with groanings too deep for words. I also cannot begin to describe you and how much you mean to me. But I do know this: I need you to be my refuge in the storm today. I need to know you are with me. I need to understand and experience your protection, so please come near! Amen.*

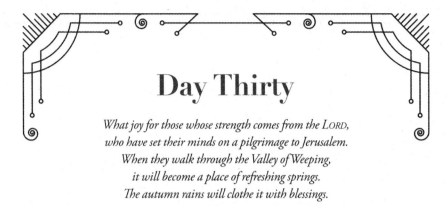

Day Thirty

What joy for those whose strength comes from the LORD,
who have set their minds on a pilgrimage to Jerusalem.
When they walk through the Valley of Weeping,
it will become a place of refreshing springs.
The autumn rains will clothe it with blessings.

PSALM 84:5-6

Joy comes in the midst of our pain; it's one of the things God loves to provide for us, particularly when our lives are falling apart.

The psalmist here speaks of a pilgrimage, a journey toward Jerusalem, which served as the spiritual center of worship for Jewish people during that time. On their way to worship God, the people described in this passage walk through a long, sad valley—a barren place of drudgery. And yet, God shows up in the midst of the trek, turning what was once a sad pilgrimage into a refuge, full of refreshment.

That's God's heart for you as you walk through your own "Valley of Weeping." What a perfect metaphor for the healing journey! We weep. We trudge. We question. We grow weary. The road never seems to end, even after our supply of water terminates. We see Jerusalem, the place of worship, on the horizon, but we feel more like we're walking on a treadmill, taking many steps, but never advancing. Thirst overcomes. Tears become our companions. And we lose heart.

And yet, we seek a God who loves to resurrect, don't we? When the journey leads to what looks like yet another dead end, God brings life. We see in the New Testament that Jesus calls the Holy Spirit "living water" (John 7:38-39). God gives to all who thirst along the way, and the refreshment he brings is of a permanent kind. It's interesting to note that when Jesus talks of living water in John 4, he speaks to a Samaritan woman who wonders which mountain to worship God

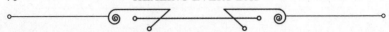

on—their mountain or Jerusalem. Jesus's point is that it isn't the mountain, but God himself who can be found along the journey (see verses 20-24).

Are you thirsty, weary, and travel-worn? Do you need joy today? Has the Valley of Weeping loomed larger to you than the heights of Jerusalem? Take heart. Your God will refresh you. He will provide springs of water. He will shower you with the kind of rain that ushers forth growth and blessings. Though I know it's desperately hard to trust God when you've experienced tremendous hurt, he will, over time, prove himself trustworthy as you walk along the healing journey. Don't give up.

Jesus, I am so tired of walking through the Valley of Weeping. I'm thirsty. I have blisters. I can't seem to make progress. I lack joy. In fact, I want to just give up. But these verses remind me that you will walk with me in my pilgrimage. You will empower me to take the next step. You will be the living water I so desperately need. I believe! But please help my unbelief. Amen.

Day Thirty-One

*Those who plant in tears
will harvest with shouts of joy.
They weep as they go to plant their seed,
but they sing as they return with the harvest.*

PSALM 126:5-6

Healing is excruciating, and it takes a lot longer than we ever hope. But there is great benefit to the healing journey. We plant our grief in the soil of expectation. We weep as we plunge a seed of aspiration into the soil. And then we wait, and often the waiting means more tears, more prayer, more frustration.

The person who makes a living from the land intrinsically understands the rhythm of this wait. There is a time of desolation (winter) where nothing seems to grow. From outward circumstances, this appears to be true. All is dead. All is quiet. Stark limbs stretch in vain to a pale, opaque sky. Green is gone, replaced by black, white, and gray.

Our spring season brings with it the promise of rain (more tears!) and hope. All that once seemed lost and dead has gloriously given up the charade and dared to poke life through the soil. Summer reminds us that fruit still happens and all that heartache has meaning as we gnaw on a juicy peach. And autumn hearkens back to harvest imagery, ripe grains, ready fields, and happy farmers.

The healing journey is long. It has seasons. And tears are the water your heart needs to thrive. Don't despise your current place in the seasonal schedule. There will be fruit. Joy will emerge as dawn welcomes us daily. There is always, always hope.

God promises us in this passage that no tear is wasted, and he will gently enforce the rhythms of planting, growing, and harvesting in our lives. Your part is to patiently endure—every day. This is your offering

to God, your obedience that makes him smile. When you trust that a better day is coming and healing will emerge, you are showing God how you're learning the art of trust. Believing that shouts of joy and harvest-singing will come reflects the faith you have.

> *Jesus, I identify with the first part of these verses—*
> *the crying and weeping. What I want to identify*
> *with is joyful shouting and singing. Teach me to*
> *patiently endure this part of my healing journey,*
> *looking forward with anticipation to what you will*
> *do. Thank you for the seasons of my healing. Please*
> *bring me into places of harvest, I pray. Amen.*

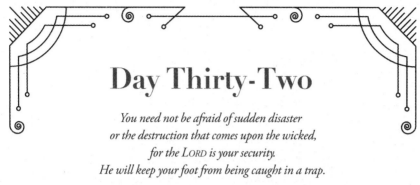

Day Thirty-Two

You need not be afraid of sudden disaster
or the destruction that comes upon the wicked,
for the LORD is your security.
He will keep your foot from being caught in a trap.

PROVERBS 3:25-26

Verses like these can either be really encouraging or entirely frustrating. And when you find them in the pages of a devotional, they tend to be the latter. We're told that God will always protect, will always prevent harm. But that's not how life ends up being, and so when we read words like this, we wonder if maybe God doesn't do what he says he does, or maybe he simply doesn't like us because he failed to protect us.

What if there was another way to process verses like this? What if we saw them as prayers for deliverance in the midst of pain rather than prayers assuring 100 percent deliverance? We are not promised an easy life. Jesus tells us we will have burdens and problems in our days, particularly if we choose to follow him. Paul assures us, "Yes, and everyone who wants to live a godly life in Christ Jesus will suffer persecution" (2 Timothy 3:12). So these verses can't be a get-out-of-problems-free card. No, they promise something better: God's presence.

The promise is this: "The LORD is your security." He is your anchor, your rock, your sure place. His presence is promised. In the Old Testament, that presence was more fleeting—where the Spirit would come on and off a person. But in the New Testament, you have a marvelous promise of continual presence. The Holy Spirit, if you are a follower of Jesus, lives with you and even within you. Wherever you walk, you bring the Spirit with you. If you walk into danger, he is there. If you cry in the middle of the night, aching over the loss of a loved one, he

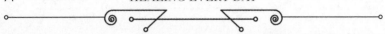

is there. If you grow weary of pursuing healing and health, he stays with you. He doesn't leave you. He doesn't forsake you. He doesn't despise your weakness. He doesn't push you away in disgust when you are needy.

No, he will always be with you. He will warn you as you walk into danger. He will provide a way of escape in temptation. He will whisper words of encouragement when your own voice shouts your unworthiness. He will be a companion when your circle of friends shrinks. You are not assured an easy life, but you are given the hope of God's presence.

Jesus, would you help me process verses like these?
Because there are times when you haven't rescued me.
I have been beaten down by this life, and I'm tired
of living in the aftermath of other people inflicting
pain on me. Yet I want to understand what it means
that you will be with me, even in the pain. Help me
remember your presence when I hurt. And instead
of blaming you when hard things happen, help me,
instead, to seek you and find you with me. Amen.

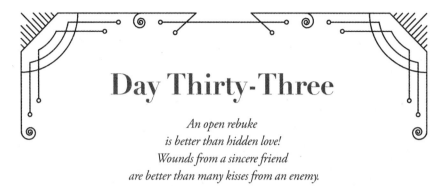

Day Thirty-Three

An open rebuke
is better than hidden love!
Wounds from a sincere friend
are better than many kisses from an enemy.

PROVERBS 27:5-6

This isn't an easy principle to applaud. We'd much rather experience hidden love or enemy kisses than rebukes and word-wounds. But as we look back on our lives, we'll know this principle holds true. It is important to have relationships in our lives with people who will be honest. It is better to welcome authentic communication than to live fakely and push away anything negative about ourselves.

How else would we ever grow? If we are left to ourselves, we will be able to carry on in our selfishness without any hindrance. We do not grow into fully joyful Christ followers in isolation. No, we grow best in community—and an honest one at that.

Look back on your life. When has someone dared to cross you in order to tell you the truth about yourself? You may not have received that "wound" easily or with joy, but after careful reflection, you realized that the words rang true. You heeded them, and your life benefited from the interaction. I once had a leader pull me aside and tell me something he saw in me—how I always felt the need to display my talents. At first, I bristled. But as I thought about it, I realized he was right. My brokenness stemmed from seldom being acknowledged as a child, so I would do anything possible to be noticed as an adult. His words launched me on a journey to understand why I did all this performing, helping me also understand my need to receive God's attention and approval first. I've seen myself not "needing" to perform since that interaction years ago.

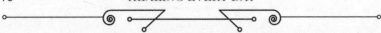

Had I pushed against his kind words (he really did deliver them kindly), I could still be ensnared to fearing what other people think, living solely for fame and acclaim. I'm grateful for the wounds of a friend. And I pray that my little story will encourage you not to retaliate when someone who loves you says something thoughtful about your journey. Take it to prayer. Consider their words. Weigh them. They may just be the catalyst you need to begin on a new avenue of healing this year.

Jesus, I pray you would empower me to keep my words to myself when someone confronts me or tells me something I'd rather not hear about myself. Help me take their words to you, to sift through them. I trust that you will show me what needs to be discarded and what needs to be considered. Please bring me honest friends who will help me see where I am and where I need to seek further healing. Amen.

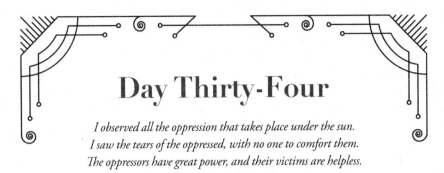

Day Thirty-Four

I observed all the oppression that takes place under the sun.
I saw the tears of the oppressed, with no one to comfort them.
The oppressors have great power, and their victims are helpless.

ECCLESIASTES 4:1

Have you ever felt the weight of these verses? If you're reading this book, I'm sure you have. When we've been harmed by narcissistic, sociopathic, or psychopathic people, we wonder why they never seem to get caught. We wonder why we encounter hundreds of victims in our lifetime. We wonder why the fight against abuse sometimes feels like leveling a mountain one teaspoon at a time.

The author of Ecclesiastes wonders the same things. He laments our broken, fallen world, and he borders on feeling helpless against the onslaught of power. Keep in mind that Solomon, the book's author, chased everything he could to fill his heart—and ended up empty. Even if you fight for justice, you'll inevitably crash into the truth that perpetrators seem to flourish. Therefore, the pursuit of justice can never ultimately satisfy the human heart when the world's in the state it's in.

But there is hope, friend. While it's true that those who prey on innocents seem to "get away" with it, the truth is, they won't. God sees. He knows. Nothing escapes his notice. While some may flourish in their evil perpetrations on earth, they will ultimately not prevail in the hereafter.

When my heart is filled with dark thoughts, and I've lamented how often evil triumphs, I have to remind myself that this earth is only part of the divine story. Perfect justice will prevail in the end. The wrongs will be righted. The broken will be restored. The old will be made new. Those who spend their lives on evil pursuits without repenting will

experience retribution. And only God is capable of enacting perfect justice. Rest there, even if evil seems to run amok today.

> *Jesus, I don't understand why bad people get away with their heinous acts, seemingly day after day, year after year. Where is the penalty? Where is justice? Instead of me feeding off this injustice, help me use that energy to turn my full attention to you—the perfect judge. Help me rest my angst in your capable hands today. I know that when I try to take vengeance, my heart grows bitter. Instead, I choose to trust you. Amen.*

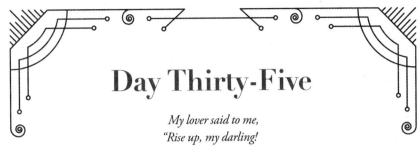

Day Thirty-Five

My lover said to me,
"Rise up, my darling!
Come away with me, my fair one!
Look, the winter is past,
and the rains are over and gone.
The flowers are springing up,
the season of singing birds has come,
and the cooing of turtledoves fills the air."

SONG OF SOLOMON 2:10-12

Solomon wrote this book in celebration of his lover, though some interpreters say the discourse echoes God and his people. Regardless of how you read it, the message it conveys is one of hope. You may remember what life felt like in the throes of young love. Everything in your teen years felt important. Every emotion carried the deepest weight. Your sadness reached the depths of woe, while your joys flew heavenward.

As you grew older, you realized the fickleness of emotions, and you learned to moderate them. In other words, you learned how to talk to your heart. When you experienced the depths, you reminded yourself that the sadness would eventually pass. When you walked through elation, you reveled in the moment, but didn't expect it to last forever. Maturity will do that to a person.

While it's not entirely helpful to be artificially positive, today's verses do give us a vocal blueprint for how we can remind ourselves to persevere when daily trials loom. Like the lover speaking hope to his beloved, we can remind our souls that winter will pass. Spring will come. Birds will harmonize. The rhythm of life dictates that.

Maybe you find yourself today in the midst of cold, hard winter.

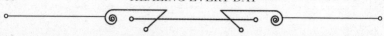

No birds sing, simply because they've flown to warmer places. No blooms scent your path because the temperatures won't allow it. But that doesn't mean you'll never experience new life again.

Reminding yourself that good will come reframes the way you look at today. Yes, today is hard. Yes, life feels stagnant. Yes, injustice currently prevails. But you serve a God of hope and renewal. You serve the God of the resurrection. Life will not always be death and sadness. Your life has great potential, through his Spirit, to become full of passion and joyfulness. So today, reframe your grief. Remind yourself that God loves to bring beauty from cold, hard ground. Then wait in anticipation for what is next.

Jesus, like Solomon spoke to his beloved, help me remind myself today that all this sadness does not have to last. I choose to rest in knowing you will bring good things my way. I pray you'd help me endure this season with joy. Give me hope in the midst of loss and cause my heart to anticipate what you will do next. I need that kind of life, Jesus. Amen.

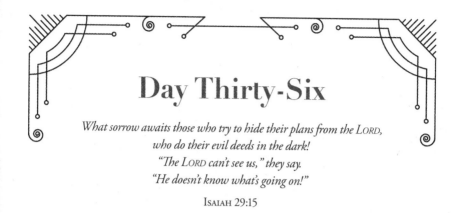

Day Thirty-Six

What sorrow awaits those who try to hide their plans from the LORD,
who do their evil deeds in the dark!
"The LORD can't see us," they say.
"He doesn't know what's going on!"

ISAIAH 29:15

What a relevant verse for those who have survived heartache. There are times when we wonder when justice will come. For me? I'd been haunted for years by the sexual assault I experienced from two teenage boys when I was five. And I spent a lot of time trying to discern their identity. Thankfully, I didn't find out any relevant information until I was ready to handle it. In a series of events that can only be described as miraculous, some sleuths uncovered one name. A man who had died of cancer years prior.

Though they couldn't uncover the other perpetrator, this felt like enough for me. I'd spent a great deal of time worrying that those two men continued to hurt others, but since the one had passed, I no longer had to fret—at least in terms of him. Prior to the discovery of his name, though, I did hold on to verses like today's. I knew that God saw all that happened to me. He took note of the abuse. He would not forget it.

I don't know if those two ever met Jesus on earth. I don't know if they repented, bowing hearts and knees and wills to him. I don't know if they begged God for forgiveness or deeply regretted what they did. But I can know that God knows all. And he will deal with each of us justly.

That's why, as survivors of pain, we need to have a robust theology of heaven. We must remember that what we see here on a sin-marred earth is not all there is. Justice may not happen here, but it will happen there. God will make all things right. He will judge perfectly. He

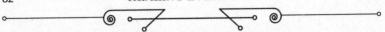

will grant mercy to those who have bowed before him on earth. And he will bring judgment on those who wrongly felt they got away with harming others.

When you're walking through this kind of grief, remember the name Hagar gave God: *El Roi*, "the God who sees" (Genesis 16:13). He sees you. He sees them. He sees all. Rest in that. Trust in that. Be still. Heaven will contain perfect justice, and you will experience the fulfillment of all that healing you've been seeking so diligently on earth.

> *Jesus, help me remember that you see everything. You know. You watch. Nothing escapes your notice, even though some folks seem to get away with hurting many. I'm grateful I'm not the judge. Today, I choose to think on heaven, to remember that you will make all things right and new. Would you remind me today that you also see me? I need to know you're mindful of me and my sometimes-frustrating healing journey. Amen.*

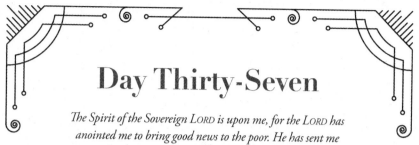

Day Thirty-Seven

The Spirit of the Sovereign LORD is upon me, for the LORD has anointed me to bring good news to the poor. He has sent me to comfort the brokenhearted and to proclaim that captives will be released and prisoners will be freed. He has sent me to tell those who mourn that the time of the LORD's favor has come, and with it, the day of God's anger against their enemies. To all who mourn in Israel, he will give a crown of beauty for ashes, a joyous blessing instead of mourning, festive praise instead of despair. In their righteousness, they will be like great oaks that the LORD has planted for his own glory.

ISAIAH 61:1-3

This is a longer passage of Scripture than you'll normally read in *Healing Every Day*, but I felt it was important to include the entire thought. Here, the prophet Isaiah shares what God has done on his behalf and how he's become a spokesperson of healing for the nation of Israel. Remember that when he is sharing these comforting words, the nation of Israel will experience exile in the future. He is preparing them for the coming ordeal. Not only that, he's also reminding the Israelites that they, too, can look beyond what they suffer to a new day of wholeness.

Doesn't that resonate with those of us on the healing journey? Like the nation of Israel, we have encountered many trials in the past. We experienced a lack of freedom, and at times, walked through harsh treatment. We currently have mountains to face, and the future will also hold its own unknowns. But eventually, we will experience pervasive and complete healing.

As we walk this healing road, the words of Isaiah serve as a promise of the now and the not yet. We will experience good news, comfort,

release, freedom, favor, beauty, blessing, praise, and righteousness. We may not experience these things completely, but we will taste them on this earth—a sure sign that God is with us.

The last part of this passage reminds us of something entirely beautiful. We will be like oaks of righteousness, tall, strong, immovable. As God heals bits and pieces of us along the way, we grow deeper roots, and our branches reach heavenward. Although the entirety of your healing cannot yet happen on earth, you always have the opportunity to grow and reach and thrive.

> *Jesus, I needed this reminder today that you are healing me along the way. I do want to be a strong tree that withstands the storms of life. I need your good news, comfort, release, freedom, favor, beauty, blessing, praise, and righteousness today. I need to know you are with me. And I choose to hope that all things will be made new (including me) when everything culminates at the end of the age. Amen.*

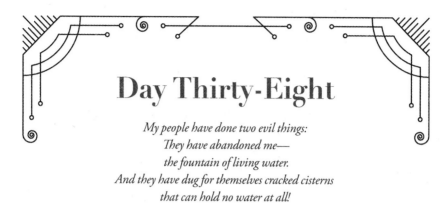

Day Thirty-Eight

My people have done two evil things:
They have abandoned me—
the fountain of living water.
And they have dug for themselves cracked cisterns
that can hold no water at all!

JEREMIAH 2:13

When we're hurt, we tend to dig cisterns. Our first desire isn't to turn to God, but to chase anything we can control—which is why digging cisterns is a good metaphor.

What is a cistern? It's a container or hole in the earth that collects and holds rainwater. If it's in proper working order, it captures, then dispenses life-giving water to people, their crops, and their animals. But when a cistern is broken, it becomes worthless, acting more like a sieve than a container because the water runs right through.

Even if you have a properly working cistern, the water will never be fresh. In fact, it's in danger of stagnating or holding parasites and disease-causing pathogens.

Contrast this with the living water Jesus promises us in John 4. He is that source of ever-living water, and it does not stagnate or bring death. In fact, it can only sustain life.

Why is it that we chase after stagnation instead of running to Jesus? The answer lies in that seven-letter word *control*. When we're hurt, we retreat into ourselves. Maybe relational chaos reigns around us, and the only thing we can think to do is hunker down and make something happen. When we're hurting, we realize we can't control others, so we shift to anything we can control. And then we wonder why it all falls apart.

Instead of control, choose surrender today. Surrender to Jesus and

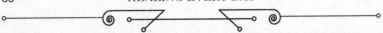

his ways. Trust that he will provide the living water you need to be sustained. Remember that when he offers help, it comes with peace, not discord. And when he offers refreshment, he does so without shame. He freely gives you what will quench your thirst. And although others hurt you, you can rely on the fact that Jesus will never abandon you, particularly when you're mourning a broken relationship.

Jesus, when someone hurts me, help me run to you, the fountain of living water. I grow tired of digging holes that don't actually work and often just make me tired and sick. Instead of trying so hard to handle everything on my own, empower me to surrender, to let you lead me, to receive all the living water you want to give me. Amen.

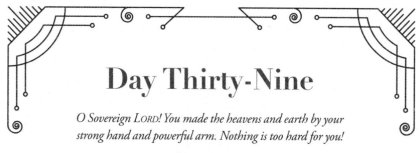

Day Thirty-Nine

O Sovereign LORD! You made the heavens and earth by your strong hand and powerful arm. Nothing is too hard for you!

JEREMIAH 32:17

This particular scripture was put to music decades ago in a praise song, and for whatever reason, the chorus reverberates through me whenever I'm going through a stressful situation. It reminds me that God is bigger than the mountain I face, whether that mountain be something I'm anticipating that will be hard or the past hurt I'm trying to heal from today. Nothing is too difficult for God. Nothing.

Because he created the world we live in with a word, we can trust that he is intimately acquainted with our ways (see Psalm 139). He knows when we lie down and stand up. He knows when we eat. He knows the crazy lies we believe in our heads about our worth. He sees us when we're suffering. He notices our heartache. He even sees the unseen—where we quietly struggle for significance in the aftermath of pain.

If he can spin the world into life (and he did), he can surely come to your aid. This is the kind of truth you can found your life on. It is solid and unswerving.

But perhaps the chaos you've experienced pushes against this idea of a capable, strong God. Maybe you've wondered if God is weak because he didn't rescue you in the way you would've wanted. Maybe you are trying desperately *not* to question God in the stillness of your thoughts because you feel that would be unkind. Yet, the questions continue. They birth new questions. And you berate yourself for a lack of faith.

God already knows your questions. He knows your doubts. He understands that you can't possibly understand the mystery of his ways. His ears are utterly capable of hearing your cries, worries, frustrations,

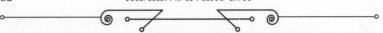

and even anger toward him. He loves you as you are. But he is also strong on your behalf. That mountain you're facing? He's bigger. That fear that's immobilizing you? He's bigger. That broken relationship beyond repair? He's bigger. That plan he is unfolding? Bigger and more creatively different than you can imagine.

Jesus, I want to remember today that nothing is too difficult for you. But I have to admit I have questions about that. I've seen times in my life when you haven't rescued me. I have experienced heartache that I don't understand. Why did you allow it? Thank you that you love me even when I'm honest with you about my disappointments. Please, please move the mountains that loom before me. And empower me to realize again that nothing is too difficult for you. Amen.

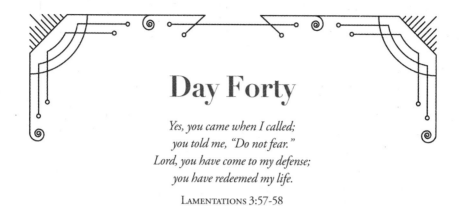

Day Forty

Yes, you came when I called;
you told me, "Do not fear."
Lord, you have come to my defense;
you have redeemed my life.

LAMENTATIONS 3:57-58

J eremiah penned these words to God in the midst of many difficult circumstances in his tumultuous prophetic life. Called the "weeping prophet," he had the painful distinction of prophesying about Jerusalem's destruction and Judah's inevitable exile. He experienced several death threats, mockery, abandonment, and ridicule. And yet, his perseverance and tenacity served not only to warn the Israelites of what would come (in the book of Jeremiah), but his words in both Jeremiah and Lamentations are preserved for us to read and gain strength from today.

He reminds those of us who have also suffered that God comes to our aid when we call upon him. And as New Testament believers, we have the immediacy of the Holy Spirit within us whenever we feel afraid or tense.

Jeremiah must've experienced profound fear, particularly when he uncovered a plot by his countrymen to kill him (Jeremiah 11:18-19), or when enemies lowered him into a muddy cistern to die (Jeremiah 38:6). Based on today's verse, at some point he reminded himself of God's steady words: "Do not fear."

After God rescues Jeremiah from peril, he affirms the goodness of God. He concentrates on the ability of God to not only defend him, but to redeem what had been taken from him.

When you face a particularly difficult relational trial, remember

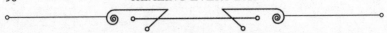

these sure tenets from Jeremiah: Call on God. Trust his nearness. Do not fear. Rest in God's rescue and redemption.

While we may not face the extreme persecution and backlash Jeremiah did, we do suffer on this earth. And we reel in the aftermath of attack and pain. Even so, it's good for us to call on God, trust his good intent, and wait humbly for him to rescue and redeem what's been lost. This takes patience and perseverance. It takes reminding ourselves of the truth of God's unchanging character. It takes choosing to step toward health when we'd rather mask the pain or run away. Today, you have that choice. Press in and trust, or shove down and flee. Which will you choose?

> *Jesus, thank you that Jeremiah endured such hardship and penned such encouraging words for me. Please be near when I call on you. Teach me the art of living without fear. Rescue me. Redeem what's been lost in my life. Give me the gumption needed to face my pain and trust you for outcomes rather than shoving down the pain and running away from it. Oh, how I want to heal today! Amen.*

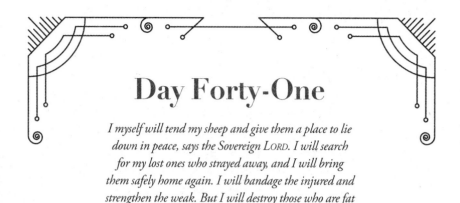

Day Forty-One

*I myself will tend my sheep and give them a place to lie
down in peace, says the Sovereign* LORD. *I will search
for my lost ones who strayed away, and I will bring
them safely home again. I will bandage the injured and
strengthen the weak. But I will destroy those who are fat
and powerful. I will feed them, yes—feed them justice!*

EZEKIEL 34:15-16

Here we see an image of a shepherd who attends those entrusted
to him. It's beautiful to realize this is God speaking to his people
about his caretaking role in their lives. When Jesus shares the parable
of the prodigal son in Luke 15, we see this type of loving-kindness displayed as the father waits in anticipation for the return of his son—a
lost sheep if there ever was one. He doesn't berate the son or push him
away. No, he welcomes him back into the fold and celebrates his return.

Good shepherds act this way. They tend their flock, provide tran-
quil pastures in which to eat and rest, seek to find the lost or stray ones,
and return them "safely home." What a beautiful picture of a God who
cares for us.

But there is more in this passage for those of us who are walking
the healing path: God not only provides for us and rescues us when we
stray, but he also bandages our wounds and empowers us when we're
weak. What a poignant snapshot of God's tender care. He doesn't push
us away. He doesn't berate us for being injured. He doesn't kick us
when we're down. He doesn't blame us when we're hurt. He bandages.
He takes gentle care of us.

You might be tempted to forget the very last portion of today's passage, but don't gloss over it. Why? Because it reminds us that while God
cares for us in our most vulnerable state, he is also aware of injustice.

And not only that, he does something about it. Inevitably, God will take to task those who hurt others. He sees it all. He will enact justice.

If we served a God who only cared for the broken, but did not care about justice, our world would be far more broken than it already is. This passage reminds us to trust in the personal attention of God—both for the victim and the perpetrator. Neither goes unnoticed.

Jesus, thank you that you are a good shepherd who chases after the straying one, bandages wounds, and gives strength to those who no longer have any left. I am that sheep, desperately in need of your care. I need some calm pastures and peaceful valleys. But I'm also grateful that those who perennially take advantage of the weak will not ultimately prevail. Thank you that you are also the God of justice. Amen.

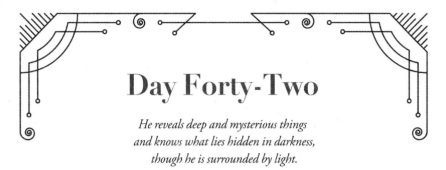

Day Forty-Two

*He reveals deep and mysterious things
and knows what lies hidden in darkness,
though he is surrounded by light.*

DANIEL 2:22

When darkness overcrowds your life and you cannot see any light at all, remember this: God is light, and he is surrounded by it. He cannot *not* be light. He always overcomes the darkness because it is in his nature to do so. He can't help but shine.

Since he created the world with a word, he understands mysteries we cannot fathom. Since he separated light and darkness, and he himself was the light of earth before he flung the sun and moon and stars into existence, he knows how to govern with light. When we flip to the end of the Bible, we see the new heavens and the new earth, a revitalized and rejuvenated creation, as it should be—bathed in his light, no sun necessary. God's light is sure. It is real. It cannot be extinguished.

When you look back on your story, chances are there are snapshots of darkness—times in your life you simply cannot understand, discern, or maybe even fully remember. Even if you never understand all of your story this side of eternity, you can rest in knowing God does.

For a long time, I've had a hole in my memory when (I've been told) I was homeless as a young child. I've asked God many times to enlighten me, to help me remember. But so far, he has not granted that request. I had to come to the place where I realized that he knew what was best for me on this healing journey, and that perhaps this story is masked for a reason. On the other side, when God's light penetrates everything, and he wipes all the tears from my eyes, I will finally have that "aha" moment of understanding. Until then, I trust the God of light to shed light on my path, little by little.

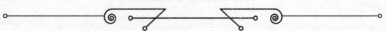

While it may be frustrating that parts of our stories remain mysterious, there is solace in remembering that God holds everything in his hands for the proper timing. I'm now grateful that I didn't start working through my own story until after I met him. And even then? I would have shrunk back had he shined a light on all I'd have to walk through in the coming years. I've learned God is a gentle healer, wooing us along the path with snippets of light—just as often as we can handle them.

> *Jesus...oh, how I needed to read this today. Thank you that you are light. Thank you that no darkness dwells in you. Thank you that you sometimes mask parts of my story until I can handle those details. Thank you for being a gentle healer, giving me only what I can properly tolerate at the time. I'm grateful that one day, on the other side, I will experience the full force of your beautiful light. Until then, help me keep pursuing healing. Amen.*

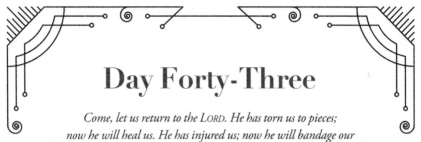

Day Forty-Three

*Come, let us return to the LORD. He has torn us to pieces;
now he will heal us. He has injured us; now he will bandage our
wounds. In just a short time he will restore us, so that we may
live in his presence. Oh, that we might know the LORD!
Let us press on to know him. He will respond to us as surely as
the arrival of dawn or the coming of rains in early spring.*

HOSEA 6:1-3

When life gets difficult, we have choices. We can either get angry that God allowed such pain and flee from him, or we can press in to know him better through the pain. So often, I choose to flee. I wonder, *How can I trust a God who allows such suffering?* But the fleeing usually doesn't last for long because I miss his presence, need his reassurances, and covet his healing. In short, I need him.

The prophet Hosea is speaking to the nation of Israel, which has long disobeyed and run away from their God. He offers a respite of hope in these words—a glorious invitation full of grace and beckoning. Hosea reminds us that God is patient; he is loving; he is waiting for us. And when we choose to return, open arms await.

We may never understand the theology of suffering while we walk this earth. It's hard to know whether our pain comes from other people's choices, a fallen world, the evil schemes of Satan and his henchmen, our own straying, or the chastisement of the Almighty. But we can know that God will redeem our pain. He, like it says in this passage, is a bandager and restorer. He takes what has been broken and makes it whole again. That is my prayer for you—for a connected wholeness to your creator.

Hosea ends this promise with metaphors from nature—assured stories that happen with the seasons. The dawn arrives every morning.

Rains water the earth in early spring in anticipation of new growth. These are bedrock, natural truths. Just as the sun rises and the clouds spit rain, we can rely on the nearness of our God. He hears us. He will listen to us. And he responds to our needs on a regular, welcoming basis. Press in to know him today. Let his welcoming become your joy.

Jesus, thank you that you don't turn away when I call to you. Thank you for bandaging my wounds and providing redemption in the midst of my struggle. You are good. Forgive me for running away when suffering has increased. Teach me, instead, to run to you for solace when the world spins out of control. Thank you that your presence is as assured as the sun rising this morning. Rain your blessings on me—your presence, my peace, and renewed hope. Amen.

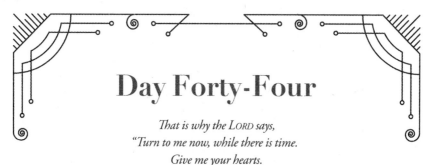

Day Forty-Four

That is why the LORD says,
"Turn to me now, while there is time.
Give me your hearts.
Come with fasting, weeping, and mourning.
Don't tear your clothing in your grief,
but tear your hearts instead."
Return to the LORD your God,
for he is merciful and compassionate,
slow to get angry and filled with unfailing love.
He is eager to relent and not punish.

JOEL 2:12-13

What a beautiful invitation to those who are broken. He asks us to return to him, to learn how to trust him even when our hearts are hurting. God's response will be based on his nature, something we can misconstrue in our pain. When we are hurting, we tend to think negatively of others, especially God. We begin to believe the world is against us, and we assign sinister motives to everyone. We push away those who want to help us, thinking they're intending harm instead of good.

When I was a child, my family returned home from a Thanksgiving celebration. Our dog, a sweet German shepherd mix who was friendly to a fault, sat on our back porch. She seemed hunched over. When I approached her, she snapped at me, growling. Upon closer inspection, we realized she'd been shot. She endured surgery, a pin, and then eventual amputation of the limb. She continued to be sweet natured—the only time she ever threatened to hurt us was when she was desperately wounded. No matter what we did, we could not convince her our intentions were good.

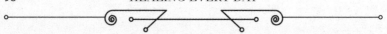

We get this way after tragedy. We assume the worst about everyone, including God. After all, he could have stopped it, right? And how are we to know he won't harm us again? Like my family's German shepherd, we assume everyone has a gun.

Joel gently reminds Judah (and us as well) that God is not what we negatively project upon him. He is merciful, not merciless. Compassionate, not callous. Slow to anger, not hotheaded. Unfailingly loving, not caustically cruel. Relentless in his pardoning, not quick to punish. You may feel shot, wounded, and frightened. Your pain may be clouding your perceptions right now. But the truth is, God is good. And he loves you with the kind of love that chases after you and endures your backlash with patience.

> *Jesus, I needed to be reminded about your character today. Pain has blurred my vision of you. Instead of running from you or lashing out, I pray you'd empower me to surrender to you, pursue your heart, and experience a grand reuniting. I need you. I need your patience and love and pardon. Free me to rest in you. Help me not to recoil at your tenderness. Instead, show me afresh that you are for me. Amen.*

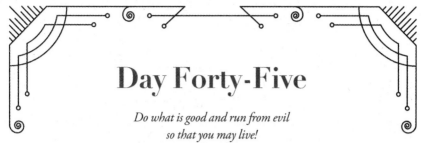

Day Forty-Five

Do what is good and run from evil
so that you may live!
Then the LORD God of Heaven's Armies will be your helper,
just as you have claimed.
Hate evil and love what is good;
turn your courts into true halls of justice.
Perhaps even yet the LORD God of Heaven's Armies
will have mercy on the remnant of his people.

AMOS 5:14-15

You may be noticing a thread of similarity in the past few passages. Remember, all these were written by the minor prophets, and their messages to God's people have similar pleas: Flee from evil. Pursue the Lord. Return to him. Trust his character. Wait patiently for restoration.

But this particular admonition has an interesting extra element to it: "Turn your courts into true halls of justice." When we choose to do good and hate evil, when we pursue justice, we experience more of God's heart. I've seen this to be true in my own journey of healing. The greatest joys I've experienced in my life come from helping others be set free. When I pivot my focus away from my pain and concentrate instead on helping others walk through theirs, I touch deeper levels of joy. This is the pursuit of justice Amos points to here.

To pursue justice is to look back on your own story of abuse, decide that this evil should not prevail in our world, then do something about it. For me, it means advocating for sexual abuse victims, lending my voice to the story, listening to others' stories, and praying for many. My little part of the justice equation ushers in further healing—something I hadn't anticipated.

Yes, you will need to walk a pathway of healing before you pursue

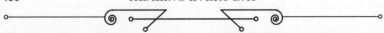

justice work. We must do the work we ask others to do, after all. But when you've experienced new levels of freedom, you'll begin to sense God nudging you out into the unknown, where you can be an advocate of justice for the voiceless. And when you take that path, even though it may be terrifying, you'll understand God's mercy in ways you hadn't before. It may be scary, but the pursuit of setting things right will bring further healing.

Jesus, I am scared. I know you've asked me to be a part of your justice solution on this earth. I know you've set me free for a purpose—to bring emancipation to others. I pray you would give me strength to take the next scary step in helping others. And as I do, keep my eyes and heart open to the new ways you will bring restoration and joy to my life. I trust you. Amen.

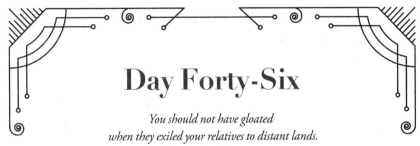

Day Forty-Six

*You should not have gloated
when they exiled your relatives to distant lands.
You should not have rejoiced
when the people of Judah suffered such misfortune.
You should not have spoken arrogantly
in that terrible time of trouble.*

OBADIAH 12

When someone hurts us or violates our trust, our minds often darken. Their offense serves as a roadblock to our recovery. When we consume ourselves with sadness because of the actions of others, we more easily fall prey to what Obadiah warns about here: gloating at our "enemy's" demise.

No good thing happens when we rejoice at another's calamity, no matter how egregious their initial offense toward us was. We have to remember that God also created the person who hurt us. He or she is an image bearer of God. He formed each person in the womb, just as he formed us. And when we take on the mantle of judge, jury, and punisher (at least in our minds), we usurp God's rightful role of justice provider.

When Jonah grew angry that God spared Nineveh after his reluctant journey of preaching through that great city, he was upset at God's goodness. No doubt when the prodigal son's brother in Jesus's parable heard the sounds of partying and revelry, he nursed this same kind of grudge. But neither person, according to the narratives, was justified in their rage.

Because of our humanity, we cannot know the intricate weavings of God's grand story. Redemption is always an option. God desires that none should perish without first knowing him. His kindness leads

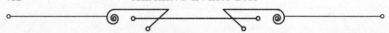

others to repentance. And sometimes, yes, our "enemies" fall beneath the weight of their sin. Sometimes they get their comeuppance. But that doesn't call for gloating. Why? Because when our soul gloats at the demise of another, it shrinks.

God's grace and beauty are available to all—even those we do not like. Instead of longing for demise (or applauding it), let's occupy ourselves with prayer for that offender. Of course, it is good to pray for justice, but it's also good for our souls to pray for mercy upon our enemies as well.

> *Jesus, I confess that when that person who hurt me finally suffered for their sin, I rejoiced. Help me turn that revelry into an acknowledgment of my own frailty and a plea for your kindness over my enemy. You tell me to love my enemies and pray for those who persecute me, so I choose to do that today. Thank you for your outrageous kindness. Without it, I am destitute. Amen.*

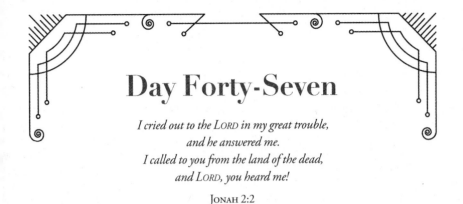

Day Forty-Seven

I cried out to the LORD in my great trouble,
and he answered me.
I called to you from the land of the dead,
and LORD, you heard me!

JONAH 2:2

Prayer is one of those practices we tend to abandon when life doesn't go our way. We begin to reason that God doesn't hear, he's too busy, or he simply is bothered with us and doesn't want to act on our behalf. We imagine our prayers hitting the light fixtures, but never venturing beyond. Particularly when we've experienced far more pain than we think we can bear, our words to God quiet, and we sink into silence.

Or maybe we feel we've sinned far too much for God to welcome back our words. We've made egregious choices, and we believe that if we ask God for deliverance, our pleas will fall on deaf ears. So we stay quiet while our souls break.

Jonah could've followed that same tack. Although he experienced extreme trial, he did so because of his own rebellion. He could have let his words rest there, accepted his fate in the stomach of a big fish, and died at sea. But something within him chose to cry out. In desperation, he let God know his needs. He trusted in the goodness of God—something he would later lament when Nineveh repented and experienced God's grace.

His words here are instructive for anyone who is suffering. We can cry out to God when we face great trouble. And in the midst of that cry, God answers us. He reveals himself to us. He restores our souls to flourishing. Even when life seems over—"the land of the dead" sounds ominous indeed—we still have access to our loving, available Father. God hears every prayer, even when it's as short as "Help!"

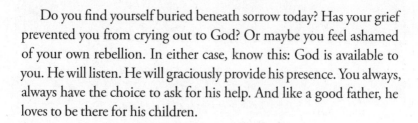

Do you find yourself buried beneath sorrow today? Has your grief prevented you from crying out to God? Or maybe you feel ashamed of your own rebellion. In either case, know this: God is available to you. He will listen. He will graciously provide his presence. You always, always have the choice to ask for his help. And like a good father, he loves to be there for his children.

> *Jesus, I'm tired. I am at the end of my pain rope. I know I haven't always cried out to you when I've been distressed, but today I choose to do so. Will you bring rescue? Will you be with me as I mourn? Will you show me that you love me? I desperately need to know that you welcome me back into your circle of friendship. Oh, how I need you today. Amen.*

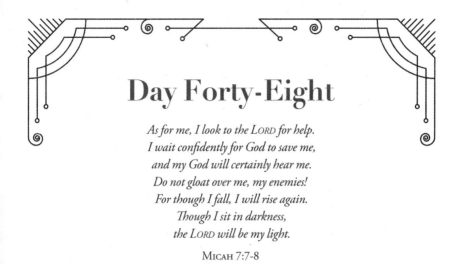

Day Forty-Eight

As for me, I look to the LORD for help.
I wait confidently for God to save me,
and my God will certainly hear me.
Do not gloat over me, my enemies!
For though I fall, I will rise again.
Though I sit in darkness,
the LORD will be my light.

MICAH 7:7-8

There are times when we read words like those above and wonder if such declarations are true for us. Will we rise again? Will God be our light in the darkness? What if death seems more likely? What if the darkness overwhelms our day?

The pivotal phrase is this: "I look to the LORD for help." Micah has made a determination, despite his current circumstances, to seek God in the midst of his pain. Not only that, but he's grown enough in his relationship with God to know that God's answers are not instantaneous. He knows that sometimes God's timing is not swift—or at least according to his agenda. So he has learned the art of waiting on God.

Note, too, that Micah doesn't say, "And God will certainly answer all my prayers according to my will, my timing, my agenda." No, he says that God will hear his prayers. We will be heard. We will have an audience with the King of kings and the Lord of lords. What God chooses to do as he unfolds his paradoxical plan is up to him, but he promises to hear us, to validate our concerns, to sit with us, and to dignify our pleas.

In light of experiencing God's presence, Micah makes declarations over his enemies. He instructs them to no longer gloat over him. We can do this as well by affirming our worth in light of the lies we've heard

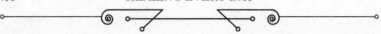

enemy-like people speak over us. We can say out loud that God loves us; he made us; and we are full of dignity and light. Nothing someone else says or does strips us of that truth.

Today, do this: Tell God everything on your heart. Then wait with confidence, knowing that he loves to be near you, to give you his presence. Declare out loud your worth, despite what others have said about you or to you. Rest in the truth that you are dearly, truly, completely loved right now.

Jesus, I confess that I don't often relish waiting to hear from you. I want you to act on my behalf yesterday! Teach me the maturity that comes from waiting on you. Train me to realize that it's your presence I need more than the answers to my prayers. Deliver me from the words others have spoken to and over me. I need to know that you love me, and that I am worthy because you made me. Amen.

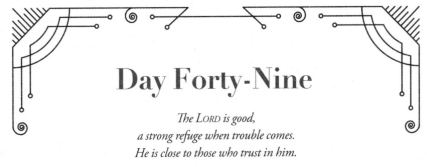

Day Forty-Nine

The LORD is good,
a strong refuge when trouble comes.
He is close to those who trust in him.

NAHUM 1:7

I remember, in terror, when the ghosts streaked the sky. I was probably seven years old, utterly alone, facing the night from inside my little home. Always prone to fear and suspicion, I automatically jumped to the conclusion that specters were out to get me. I had no frame of reference for a searchlight, most likely advertising the latest model of Chevy. Alone, I could only see the shifting light in the night sky as ominous.

Thankfully, my stepfather arrived home. He explained that the ghosts were, in fact, searchlights, and I breathed out my fear. Looking back, I see how isolation breeds fear, and that, when we're lonely and alone, our fears multiply. Those of us who have endured trauma know this instinctively. We know we need safe places with safe people in order to conquer our worry.

Sometimes, though, there are no people around when we're afraid. No one can accompany us into the MRI machine. When we're in conflict, there are times we face that alone. And when we dare to uncover the pain from the past in order to heal, it's hard to find faithful friends who will boldly walk us through it.

When we're at our most fearful, when others are not around, we can return to the promise of today's scripture. God is the one who is with us in the MRI machine. He is the God of broken relationships. He doesn't rescue us from every problem, memory, or temptation, but he does promise presence. He will be with us.

Like my stepfather, who explained away the ghosts, our Father in

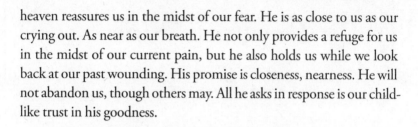

heaven reassures us in the midst of our fear. He is as close to us as our crying out. As near as our breath. He not only provides a refuge for us in the midst of our current pain, but he also holds us while we look back at our past wounding. His promise is closeness, nearness. He will not abandon us, though others may. All he asks in response is our child-like trust in his goodness.

> *Jesus, thank you for being a refuge to me. Thank you for explaining my fear, giving me context for my worry, and simply being near when I feel utterly alone. Thank you for loving me like that. I know there are times I lash out at you and push you away, but you have proven yourself kind and good and strong. I need you today. I need your hand in mine. Amen.*

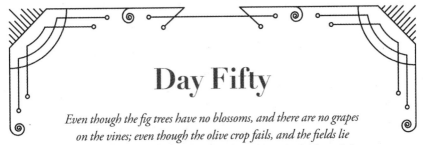

Day Fifty

Even though the fig trees have no blossoms, and there are no grapes
on the vines; even though the olive crop fails, and the fields lie
empty and barren; even though the flocks die in the fields, and the
cattle barns are empty, yet I will rejoice in the LORD! I will be joyful
in the God of my salvation! The Sovereign LORD is my strength! He
makes me as surefooted as a deer, able to tread upon the heights.

HABAKKUK 3:17-19

What a faith-filled declaration the prophet Habakkuk boldly shares. This sentiment pushes against what the prosperity gospel promises—that God wants us to always experience unlimited health and wealth and favor.

The truth is evident if we scan the world we live in, isn't it? Wars. Famine. Discord. Health crises. Broken homes. We are not promised a pain-free life. We will have trouble as we walk this earth. This is simply the reality. By admitting this truth of a fallen world, we are not being faithless; we are being honest.

Fig trees fail to blossom. Vines die, grapeless. Olive trees wither. Fields lie fallow. Livestock die. These were economic realities during Israel's time. We, too, face economic stress. Mortgages slip into foreclosure. Children are raised in poverty. There is more month than money. Our start-ups fail. And yet, Habakkuk reminds us to rejoice.

How does he describe God? As sovereign. That means God reigns supreme over this world. He created it. He provides food for ravens, and he owns the cattle on thousands of hillsides (see Psalm 50:10). He holds everything together, and he loves to be near to his people. In light of that, we can rejoice today despite our economic woes. We can place our trust in the God who rules rightly.

Yes, times of trial will come. Yes, they did happen in the past, leaving

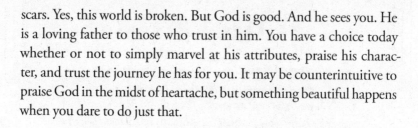

scars. Yes, this world is broken. But God is good. And he sees you. He is a loving father to those who trust in him. You have a choice today whether or not to simply marvel at his attributes, praise his character, and trust the journey he has for you. It may be counterintuitive to praise God in the midst of heartache, but something beautiful happens when you dare to do just that.

> *Jesus, I choose to praise you today. You are sovereign over all creation. You are good, even when I fear. You are my provider, not me. You are the beginning and end of my story, and you are weaving my narrative for my good and your glory. I rejoice in you. No matter what my economic reality may be, this choice to praise you is my offering. Amen.*

Day Fifty-One

I will deal severely with all who have oppressed you.
I will save the weak and helpless ones;
I will bring together
those who were chased away.
I will give glory and fame to my former exiles,
wherever they have been mocked and shamed.

ZEPHANIAH 3:19

There will be an end to your suffering.

In this particular instance, the prophet Zephaniah is speaking to the people of God. They would experience oppression. They would be weak and helpless in their coming exile. They'd be chased away from their homeland, disgraced, homeless, and hopeless. And yet, God promises to restore them. He will dignify their stories, giving them renewed purpose.

Perhaps when you read today's scripture, you could identify with the people of Judah. Digging into the past, you see where people who were tasked with protecting you became predators instead. When you were at your weakest, someone sinister took advantage of you. Maybe you were kicked out of your home. Or perhaps others bullied you, mocking you. The result of it all has been a huge dose of pain and shame, following you wherever you go.

There is hope. God sees. He carries everyone's stories, and he works to redeem them. He takes away shame. He bears the weight of mockery. He releases those in bondage.

But sometimes it's hard to believe that, particularly when we're in the midst of our pain. We can feel like an exiled nation, unseen, suffering. Yet, this passage reminds us that God is not only interested in our

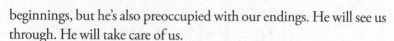

beginnings, but he's also preoccupied with our endings. He will see us through. He will take care of us.

This may not happen on earth. We see people who are martyred for their faith in Jesus. Their stories here certainly end in mockery, shame, and defeat. But their ultimate story prevails beyond the grave. When the new heavens and the new earth dawn, all will be made right. The tears, God will wipe from our eyes. The pain we endured will see its final redemption. The worry and suffering will cease.

Take heart, dear one. There will be complete justice and restoration. Hold on. Your suffering has purpose, and it matters.

Jesus, help me have an eternal perspective today. When I look around at this crazy, upside-down world where so much suffering flourishes, I get discouraged. Remind me that you are the God who brings home the exiles. You are the God who sets things aright. You are the God of reconciliation. Turn my eyes to see beyond the veil of today into eternity, when everything will finally make sense and my suffering will end. Amen.

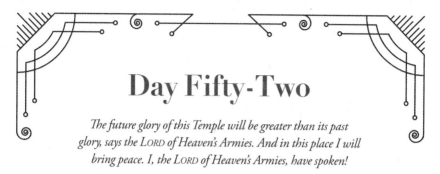

Day Fifty-Two

The future glory of this Temple will be greater than its past glory, says the LORD of Heaven's Armies. And in this place I will bring peace. I, the LORD of Heaven's Armies, have spoken!

HAGGAI 2:9

Living eschatologically means thinking and existing in light of eternity. This verse in Haggai hints at what will come beyond our lifetimes. But there is more.

Throughout the grand narrative of Scripture, God has an amazing plan of redeeming not only humankind, but creation as well. The temple in the Old Testament was a hint or foreshadowing of what Jesus would do and be. (When he died, the veil in the temple tore in two, showing that beautiful access to God the Father had been won; see Matthew 27:50-51.)

In the book of Revelation, we see everything circle back around. There's a garden (like Eden) and a city (like Jerusalem), and the presence of God representing the Temple. Just like we see in the creation account, God gives light to the new world. But there is no longer a need for sun and moon, because God himself is the light (see Revelation 21:23). Lions and lambs live in harmony. And we no longer have tears, heartache, or pain. As God promises in the Haggai passage, we will finally experience *shalom* (God's wholeness and peace all wrapped up together) every minute of every day for all eternity.

In today's world, *shalom* is granted by the Prince of Peace, Jesus— right in the midst of our trials. But there will be a time when we experience harmony all the time. God will reconcile enemies; wars will cease; families will experience restoration. That's why it's so important to think forwardly about our lives. Yes, today you are experiencing heartache. There are desires yet to be fulfilled. Some of your relationships

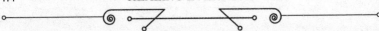

are desperately broken. But there will be a time, beyond death's shores, where God promises to make everything perfectly right.

The fact that you are longing right now for justice is proof that God has created the concept of justice. And in that longing, God draws you toward the eventual beautification of humanity and this earth. Persevere, friend. Yes, today is hard, but there will be a moment—a flash—when you will awake on the other side, completely whole, completely joyful, completely at peace.

> *Jesus, I need* shalom *right now. But I also understand there will come a day when everything is set back to rights. Thank you for placing in me that longing for justice. Thank you that it helps prove your existence. In the meantime, as I wait for what is next beyond the grave, would you give me the strength I need today to keep moving forward in the midst of my trials? I so need to know you are with me. Amen.*

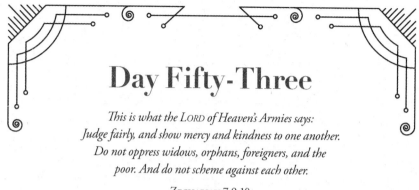

Day Fifty-Three

This is what the LORD of Heaven's Armies says:
Judge fairly, and show mercy and kindness to one another.
Do not oppress widows, orphans, foreigners, and the
poor. And do not scheme against each other.

ZECHARIAH 7:9-10

Seeing God's intent for humanity helps us who are suffering. His desire is that mankind would judge accurately, never showing favoritism or bowing down to bribery or corruption. His hope is that we would shed our eagerness for judgment and revenge and instead show mercy to those who are broken. Instead of retaliation, God longs for us to be kindhearted.

He has a special place in his heart for those who have been marginalized by society. All these—widows, orphans, foreigners, the poor—have very real economic realities that batter them incessantly. They are disadvantaged, and because of that, God's heart is bent their way. And he asks us to act in a similar way, to bend our hearts toward the downtrodden.

We serve a merciful, seek-out-the-outcast God. He is for the broken, on the side of the disadvantaged. Chances are, if you're reading this devotional about healing, you've identified with some of these people God chases after. Just watching Jesus in the Gospels, we see this tendency. He gravitated not toward the religious elite nor those who seemed to have it all together. No, he hung out with ordinary, unpretentious people. He went out of his way to dignify a bleeding woman, a leper, a blind man, a crippled person. He sought out such people.

That picture of Jesus serves as a beautiful encouragement to you today. Do you know how much Jesus loves you? Seeks you? Dignifies you? Listens to you? When you were oppressed and harmed, it hurt

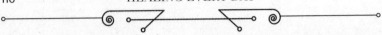

him as well. When you were overlooked, he felt that pain. When you were uninvited, he understood.

These verses remind us of two important truths: God finds the lonely and broken and pours into them, *and* he asks us to be like him in this world—doing the exact same thing. Often, our healing comes when we look beyond our own pain to help someone else in the midst of their trying story. We now have the privilege of being the hands and feet of Jesus in this difficult world, and as we serve the downtrodden, God heals more of our hearts and brings deeper joy.

> *Jesus, I pray you'd empower me to see better—to really see those people whom our society deems as unworthy or broken or deserving of being overlooked. I want to learn the art of serving others because I know it's the right thing to do, and I also realize there's a beautiful side benefit—the healing of my heart. I love you, and I want to share the love you've given me with those who are hurting today. Show me who they are. Amen.*

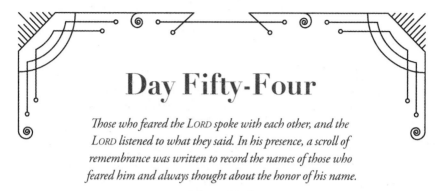

Day Fifty-Four

Those who feared the Lord spoke with each other, and the
Lord listened to what they said. In his presence, a scroll of
remembrance was written to record the names of those who
feared him and always thought about the honor of his name.

Malachi 3:16

For those who grew up feeling unknown or like an impostor, this verse gives good news indeed. If we belong to God and we pursue him wholeheartedly, our names are recorded in a scroll of remembrance. Later in the New Testament, we read about our inclusion in the book of life (see Revelation 3:5). In short, we belong to God. We are not orphans. We are not alone. We are recorded and remembered.

But so often we live as if we are orphaned. I remember very distinctly one moment in my life where I made a sad determination: only I could take care of myself. I had finally told my babysitter what two teenage boys were doing to five-year-old me. She said, "I will tell your mother." I believed her. And the next day, I naively thought that since my mother knew, I would now be safe from the rapes. But I was too young to realize that adults lie, that the babysitter hadn't told my mom, and that the boys would continue their rampage.

In that moment, I knew there existed no one on earth to swoop down and rescue me. So I learned to rescue myself by "sleeping" every afternoon. As I lay on my babysitter's large bed, curtains drawn with covers over my head for fear of being discovered not actually sleeping, I felt utterly unseen and unprotected. I certainly didn't realize God loved me.

It was only later, when I met Jesus at fifteen, that I began to understand just how precious a child is in his sight. In the Gospels, Jesus talks about the importance of children, how an adult should drown by

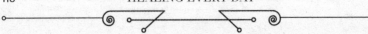

millstone if he or she causes a little one to stumble (Matthew 18:6). I began to understand my worth in light of God's love. It's not been an easy process, and it's taken me decades to wrap my mind around it, but the truth remains: I am his, and my life matters. It is recorded, and I am loved. It's the same for you, friend. You are noticed. Your name is recorded. Oh, how he loves you.

> *Jesus, help me take comfort in knowing my name is recorded and I am remembered by you. In those times of pain and isolation, remind me of that great promise. Help me preach the gospel to myself—about your life, death, and resurrection on my behalf and on behalf of all humankind. When I'm lonely, I choose to remember that you remember me. Amen.*

Day Fifty-Five

God blesses those who are poor and realize their need for him,
for the Kingdom of Heaven is theirs.
God blesses those who mourn,
for they will be comforted.

Matthew 5:3-4

This passage features such often-read words, and because of their familiarity, our hearts can gloss over deeply important truths. In the Sermon on the Mount, Jesus shakes up our view of what it means to be living in this new kingdom of heaven. It's quite upside down and counterintuitive. Poor people are blessed. Grieving people experience comfort in the midst of their mourning.

These two verses are extremely helpful for those of us who are longing for healing. Why? Because in them we realize two things: It is normal to hurt, and Jesus takes keen notice of those who do.

When you've experienced abuse in the past (or perhaps you're experiencing it right now), the last thing you think is how blessed you are, right? But Jesus reminds us that when we are at our lowest, when our strength has failed and our tears overcome our joy, he is there. He chooses to bless us with strength. Because when we are broken, we realize our need for him.

If everything went well in our lives, and we began to attribute all our success and power to our own strength, we would think we have zero need for Jesus. But because we are lacking, we know our need. And he gloriously meets it.

It's the same for those of us walking through grief. When we grieve, we acknowledge that things on this sin-filled, broken earth aren't what they are supposed to be. We have special knowledge that there will be a time when death is finally conquered, and all our grieving will turn

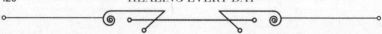

to dancing when God sets creation aright. We know there will be comfort in the future. And the beautiful thing is that God also comforts us right now.

So if you're poor, run to God who has everything. He will provide for you and give you unique glimpses into the kingdom. And if you're mourning today, let God comfort you now. Consider it his down payment on the ultimate comfort you'll experience on the other side.

> *Jesus, I needed these verses today. I needed to know that you see me in my poverty and grief. Thank you that where I am right now shows me my need for you. I cannot do this life on my own. I need you. I need your comfort and provision. I cannot trust in myself or my strength today. It is gone. But I can take the last ounce of unction in my heart and choose to trust you. Amen.*

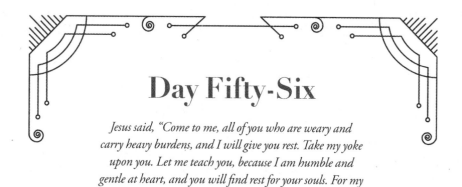

Day Fifty-Six

*Jesus said, "Come to me, all of you who are weary and
carry heavy burdens, and I will give you rest. Take my yoke
upon you. Let me teach you, because I am humble and
gentle at heart, and you will find rest for your souls. For my
yoke is easy to bear, and the burden I give you is light."*

MATTHEW 11:28-30

Oh friend, are you carrying a heavy burden today? Is it cramping your shoulders? Your soul? Your heart? How long have you been lugging it around? Who told you that you had to bear it? What benefit do you gain from keeping it heavy upon your life? The problem is this: We tend to grow so accustomed to our burdens that they become safety and familiarity to us. We get used to their weight, so much so that we cannot imagine being free of it.

Our past pain can become that kind of "friendly" burden. We believe, wrongly, that because bad things happened to us, they are now our lifelong lot. If our parents were divorced, and that separation broke us, then we consider ourselves destined to follow in our parents' footsteps and choose not to marry out of fear. If we were sexually abused, we resign ourselves to always being "messed up" in our sexuality. If we were abandoned, we expect we will always be abandoned, so we cope by building a fortress around ourselves.

When we continue to carry the burden of the past like this, our tendency is to make a solution by ourselves in our waning strength (not get married, avoid sex in marriage or overindulge, build a wall). That may work for a time, but unfortunately, it is not a permanent solution.

Jesus's invitation in these verses is this: Let the burden of the past go. Unloose the straps of the overbearing backpack filled with unresolved pain you're carrying and let it fall gloriously at the foot of the cross. You

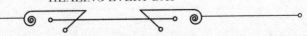

cannot fix all your pain. But you can surrender it. And in that surrender, you will find rest. Deep, needed soul rest. Give your pain to the one who bears it willingly, humbly, and beautifully.

> *Jesus, how I needed to remember this truth today. I am tired, so weary of carrying around my past. It is heavy and burdensome. I confess that I have tried to resolve my pain in my own strength, but it hasn't worked too well. Instead, I throw it all down at your feet, trusting you to take my pain. You are dependable, and I trust you to give me rest and to resolve the pain from my past. Amen.*

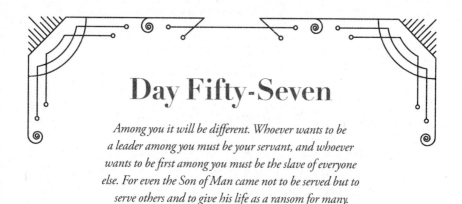

Day Fifty-Seven

*Among you it will be different. Whoever wants to be
a leader among you must be your servant, and whoever
wants to be first among you must be the slave of everyone
else. For even the Son of Man came not to be served but to
serve others and to give his life as a ransom for many.*

MARK 10:43-45

When I think of a great military leader or powerful head of government, I think of strong fists, great resolve, and power. But when I look at the world's most beloved and effective leader, Jesus, I see something entirely different. He didn't lead by brutality and strength, hands clenched in power. No, he led by example through the avenue of serving with his hands—precisely opposite of the way the world does things.

He came not to be served or revered. He didn't build a platform. He didn't infiltrate the government in order to be seen and recognized as great. He didn't force his way into the Sanhedrin, demanding an audience or humiliating the existing leaders. No, he served.

He found the broken folks like us and sat with them. He discipled many people, including Mary of Bethany, who sat at Rabbi Jesus's feet. He heard the cry of the blind man and restored his sight. He healed the legs of the paralytic lowered through the roof by hope-filled friends. When the disciples feared for their lives in the midst of stormy seas, he calmed the wind and waves. To the demonically possessed, he gave release from oppression. His lap welcomed children, and he blessed them. He so wowed the woman at the well that she became a joyful missionary to her town. He washed the disciples' feet when they should've been washing his. And in the greatest act of humble service,

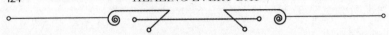

he chose to die on the cross, bearing the weight of all humanity's sin. This is our Savior, the one who serves.

When I am particularly hurting, when my past rears its ugly head and threatens to drown me, it helps me when I remember Jesus. If I walked the earth when he did, he wouldn't have pushed me away—he, the important one; me, the overlooked and needy girl. He would have served me. He would have seen me. He would have loved me. And since he is the same yesterday, today, and forever (Hebrews 13:8), he sees me (and you!) in this same way. He serves the broken, dear one. And he does not despise your brokenness.

Jesus, thank you that you came to serve and not to be served. Thank you for coming to earth not to be heralded, but to heal the broken. I am broken. I am needy. I need healing. I look back on my life and see how many times you served me by listening to me, hearing me, seeing me, and healing me. Would you continue to serve me that way? And out of supreme gratitude, I will choose to serve you and those around me who are broken too. Amen.

Day Fifty-Eight

Jesus replied, "Leave her alone. Why criticize her for doing such a good thing to me? You will always have the poor among you, and you can help them whenever you want to. But you will not always have me. She has done what she could and has anointed my body for burial ahead of time. I tell you the truth, wherever the Good News is preached throughout the world, this woman's deed will be remembered and discussed."

MARK 14:6-9

I love that Jesus welcomes people who act in unusual ways. We don't know much about this woman other than Jesus's commendation of her actions and the fact that she forsook all the shame she might receive from others to serve Jesus with heartfelt abandon. What a beautiful picture of devotion!

Perhaps you feel like your past negates your ability to worship Jesus. Maybe you worry about the religious people around you when you enter into worship. Will they sneer? Speak under their breath about your unworthiness to offer your song to God? Or maybe it's not about other people and their opinions. Maybe the sneer comes from your heart. You wonder if you're worthy of worshipping him. Living in your head, you are well aware of your own shortcomings, and this awareness may cause you to shrink back.

But the commendation here from the mouth of Jesus should give you the courage you need to worship Jesus with absolute freedom. He loves those who let go of their shame and fear, who flat out don't care what the establishment thinks because they're so in love with Jesus.

Remember, if we worship at the altar of human opinion, we will constantly live insecure lives based on what others think of us. But if we worship Jesus, not only will we find ultimate satisfaction and

acceptance, but we will also experience the commendation of our Savior. Don't let your past prevent you from wholeheartedly worshipping the one who rescued you, loves you, and has forgiven you. Your healing is astoundingly connected to your unashamed worship of him.

Jesus, sometimes I feel unworthy to come to you, to worship you, to pour out my heart before you. But you rescued me. You love me. You have wooed me to yourself. I owe you my life. So today I choose to worship you with abandon, come what may. I choose to ignore the voices of others and the bully in my head in order to fully engage in praising you for your goodness. I want to become more like you, so I choose today to worship you. Amen.

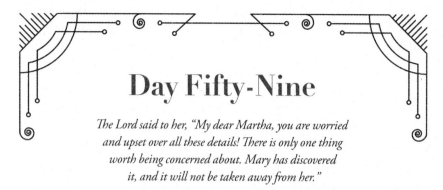

Day Fifty-Nine

*The Lord said to her, "My dear Martha, you are worried
and upset over all these details! There is only one thing
worth being concerned about. Mary has discovered
it, and it will not be taken away from her."*

LUKE 10:41-42

Although my name is Mary, I tend to be Martha-like, especially related to this interaction with Jesus and Martha. I am worried and upset far too often. Can you relate? Particularly if we've walked through trauma, we tend to have minds full of lies, broken thoughts, and shame.

There is something profoundly instructive to the abuse victim in this passage. When we redirect our angst away from our current circumstances (as Mary seems to have done) or the restless thoughts in our minds (as I try to do), and we sit at the feet of Jesus and soak him in, we find the kind of stability we long for. Why? Because Jesus does not change. His love for us is eternal; it is a truth upon which we can stake our lives.

When we choose to reorient our thoughts toward Jesus, listening to his perspective, the shouting voices in our head grow quiet. We have the space to hear life spoken over us, and in that place, the lies we've believed shrink back to their dark little corners. Spending time with Jesus in this kind of dedicated, devoted way ushers in new pathways to healing.

Recently, I've been wrestling with body image issues that stem from past sexual abuse. I have (wrongly) believed that my worth lies in the shape of my body, my appeal to the opposite sex. Although intellectually I know this is a faulty belief that will inevitably lead to heartache (and certainly not toward health), it's a hard myth to shake.

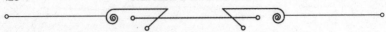

In the silence of my car yesterday, I sensed the kindness of Jesus in the midst of my struggle. He reminded me to think back through the Bible and compare how much God emphasizes our bodies versus how many times he instructs us about our hearts. In that simple phraseology from Jesus, I realized how I had majored on something he had minored on. The heart? It is the most important part of me. My body? It will fade away. But Jesus? He will remain, and his love for me is constant. That's the power of sitting at Jesus's feet. In that place of surrender, we uncover lies and steep ourselves in the truth of our belovedness.

Jesus, I don't want to spend my days captured by my own thoughts of unworthiness. I certainly don't want to live any longer believing lies about myself and the world. What I want is to know you, to sit at your feet, to hear your encouraging words spoken over me. Teach me to sit. Still my heart to listen. Calm the noise in my head. Reorient me to receive life-giving words from you. I need you today. Amen.

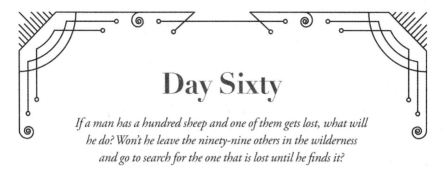

Day Sixty

*If a man has a hundred sheep and one of them gets lost, what will
he do? Won't he leave the ninety-nine others in the wilderness
and go to search for the one that is lost until he finds it?*

LUKE 15:4

Have you ever been lost? Whether we experienced the panicky angst that came when our mother's hand slipped from ours in a store, or our GPS has steered us wrong as adults, many of us have experienced lostness. It's chaotic, frightening, overwhelming.

Or have you ever experienced the lostness of someone else? Have you lost track of a friend or a child in a crowded public place? The feelings of helplessness in times like that certainly multiply.

In both cases, the lost person or the one looking for another needs this: someone in authority. A store clerk or plainclothes police officer can help discover a lost child. They will abandon their current post, going out of their way to make a mall-wide announcement. A panicked parent, upon losing a child, stops shopping and talks to someone in charge. But what would happen if the child ran away, afraid of the clerk? Or how about if a parent didn't seem to care that his child was lost? Both cases would be tragic.

Jesus is the ultimate authority. He knows when people wander off. He comforts those whose loved ones do the wandering. And his passion is to leave his station to pursue the wayward. If you have wandered, he is seeking you earnestly. If your loved one has wandered, you don't have to fear, because Jesus is searching for her and seeking her welfare.

Still, for those who have walked through trauma, it can be hard to trust Jesus. Our inclination is to think ill of anyone in authority, particularly if we've been harmed by those stronger than us. But the truth is, Jesus can be trusted. He is the God who leaves the ninety-nine happy

sheep to wander the hills and valleys in search of the one stranded, straying lamb. When he walked the earth, he demonstrated over and over his reliability and his kindhearted pursuit of those who were broken.

Maybe you're the one feeling lost today. Trauma and tragedy have pummeled you, and in your pain, you've wandered away from the very one who wants to give you life and healing. Instead of running from him, perhaps it's time to stop fleeing and grab his hand. He is searching earnestly for you.

> *Jesus, I need to know you love me today. I need to know I can trust you. I know you have authority. I know your word says you pursue the one, leaving the ninety-nine, but I'm having a hard time believing that for myself. I've been lost for so long, I don't trust anyone anymore, and I'm sure I've wrongly assigned ill motives to you. Help me be found by you. Amen.*

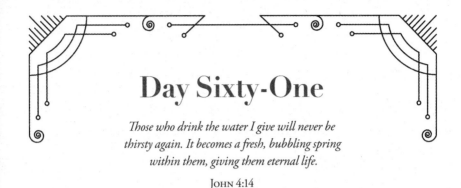

Day Sixty-One

Those who drink the water I give will never be
thirsty again. It becomes a fresh, bubbling spring
within them, giving them eternal life.

JOHN 4:14

We thirst for healing, don't we? We see others with their seemingly easy lives, and that tinge of jealousy overtakes us. Meanwhile, we continue to struggle. Sudden noises trigger us. We can't seem to let others "in." We sabotage our relationships. Or we isolate ourselves in our homes, hoping no one will spend time with us, yet longing (secretly) that they will.

Here's the truth though. One hundred percent of us struggle—even the ones who appear to have everything all together, and even those who didn't battle trauma in the past. We all bear burdens too big for us. All of us are thirsty. We are all the woman at the well, hearing these necessary words from Jesus in today's verse.

We find here that Jesus is contrasting everyday well water with the everlasting water he provides. Getting well water requires effort, and once we've dipped our bucket in the well's belly, we have to repeat that action every day until we die. We simply cannot live without water. So we draw. And we draw again.

What a perfect picture of life. Its relentlessness keeps us both humble and tired. And when we bend the metaphor toward personal growth and healing, we realize we can spend our entire lives trying in our own strength to make ourselves better. Healing, then, becomes the daily trip to the well; but the next day, we are still faced with thirst.

What would it look like to surrender? What would it benefit you to realize that the true source of healing, the true quencher of your thirst, is Jesus? What would happen if you turned over the control to him, to

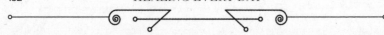

allow him to heal you in his timing, for him to bear the weight of your past pain? Jesus promises he will offer (freely!) eternal thirst-quenching. But so often, we spend so much time trying to manage our pain on our own (heading out to the well) that we miss the presence of the eternal water before us. Perhaps today's the day you surrender and take a drink of living water.

Jesus, thank you for providing the kind of thirst-quenching that outlasts my need. I know there have been times when I've tried desperately to manufacture my own healing, only to realize I need to keep coming back to my "well." Instead of being in charge of that daunting task, I choose to surrender everything to you today. I need your living water, poured out over my broken life. Please rescue me and quench my thirst for wholeness. Amen.

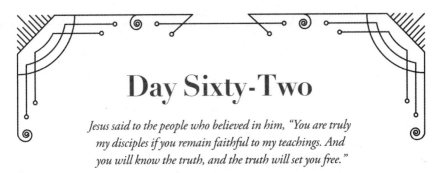

Day Sixty-Two

Jesus said to the people who believed in him, "You are truly my disciples if you remain faithful to my teachings. And you will know the truth, and the truth will set you free."

JOHN 8:31-32

Y ou've probably read this passage many, many times. But have you considered reading it from a different perspective? For those of us who have past pain, we tend to have latent lies expanding in our head. They're like cancer, multiplying. And they somehow have megaphones, growing louder by the day. The lies we've believed about ourselves drown out the truth.

Since it is true that the truth Jesus brings sets us gloriously free, it is also true that lies hold us in terrible bondage. Combatting those lies with the truth of Jesus is a necessary first step in setting your mind free. The following are some examples that may resonate with you.

Lie: I am worthless. Truth: Jesus dignified those who felt worthless when he walked the earth. Not only that, he seemed to seek them out, listening to their stories, healing their pain. And he chose to die on the cross for all of us—the strong and the weak. He valued us that much. When someone dies for you, and when that someone is the creator of the universe, you can know that your life has worth.

Lie: I am doomed to repeat the sins enacted against me. Truth: Jesus promises that we will have trouble on this earth, but he has overcome the world. He promises to bear our burdens and empower us. He sets us free from the past the moment we ask him to invade our lives. Our old lives are buried; our new lives are bursting with potential.

Lie: I deserve abandonment. Truth: Jesus will never leave or forsake you. In the Great Commission, he promised he would be with believers to the end of the age (see Matthew 28:18-20). The question of you

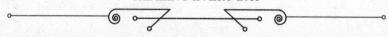

deserving or not deserving his love and presence doesn't come into play. The truth is simple: Jesus loves you, and those he loves, he never leaves.

Lie: I am beyond redemption. Truth: You are not beyond redemption. Jesus died for all of humanity, and you are one of those humans. You cannot negate your standing with him because his promise to you is based on his faithfulness, not yours.

Jesus, help me discern the lies I've believed about myself. Help me understand how those lies have kept me in bondage all these years. I want to be set free! Reveal your truths to me so I can stand against the lies. Restore my thinking. Renew my mind. I need to know you love me and you are for me. Keep me close to you today. I need to hear your voice of truth. Amen.

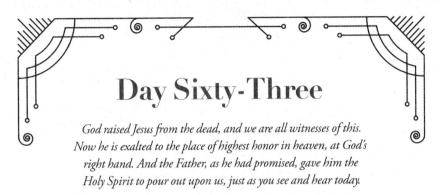

Day Sixty-Three

God raised Jesus from the dead, and we are all witnesses of this.
Now he is exalted to the place of highest honor in heaven, at God's
right hand. And the Father, as he had promised, gave him the
Holy Spirit to pour out upon us, just as you see and hear today.

<small>ACTS 2:32-33</small>

The gospel is this: Jesus lived a perfect life, died for the sins of the entire world as a perfect sacrifice, secured salvation for those who would believe, then rose again, conquering death and the grave. Because of this, you and I have hope. But there's more. He didn't just leave us with that powerful story. He also provided a way for us to live out this kingdom story the rest of our lives by graciously giving us a constant companion, the Holy Spirit.

We who have walked difficult roads know our need for help. We who have been harmed, maligned, gossiped about, physically assaulted, or sexually brutalized have great hope in Jesus. He bore the weight of all the sin committed against us as well as the sin we've pursued.

And because Jesus walked the pathway of pain in this life, he has great empathy for us who suffer. He understands abuse. He experienced nakedness in public. He felt the barb of betrayal. He was wrongly accused, spat upon, beaten. And he suffered in the mundane too—experiencing fatigue, hunger, weariness. Scripture says he wasn't handsome in appearance, but quite ordinary looking (see Isaiah 53:2). He had no political power and chose to succumb to the political and religious system that persecuted and crucified him.

He has endured so much hostility by sinners against himself (see Hebrews 12:3) that he understands when we hurt. He grieves alongside us. He "gets" personal pain. As mentioned above, his final gift to

the disciples (and to us) was granting us the presence of God through the Comforter, the Holy Spirit.

The Holy Spirit is not only a constant companion of comfort and hope, but he is also down-payment-proof that we are citizens of heaven (see 1 John 4:13). What a great heritage we have! What beautiful promises these are of God's presence today and the removal of all pain after we die. Take courage, dear one. Your God loves you, sent his Son to rescue you (and empathize with your plight), and grants the Spirit so you'll never be alone again. Rest in that truth today.

> *Jesus, how can I thank you enough for all you've done? You walked this earth so you'd understand what it's like to live here among people who hurt each other. You experienced abuse on the grandest scale, and yet you obeyed your Father. You died a criminal's death in my place, then sent your Spirit to live with me forever so I'll never be alone. Help me revisit the power of the gospel today. Amen.*

Day Sixty-Four

We can rejoice, too, when we run into problems and trials,
for we know that they help us develop endurance. And endurance
develops strength of character, and character strengthens our
confident hope of salvation. And this hope will not lead to
disappointment. For we know how dearly God loves us, because
he has given us the Holy Spirit to fill our hearts with his love.

Romans 5:3-5

You may be wondering, like I did, how many trials a person can endure. I made an unconscious determination in my twenties that went something like this: *Okay, God, I have had enough trauma and pain in my life. From now on? You owe me a perfectly joyful life, without trials, and certainly with no more pain.*

I figured God owed me, right? Except that he didn't obey my silent mandate. When I was newly married and pregnant, I found out our first pregnancy was ectopic, which meant surgery for me, the loss of a baby, and the potential loss of fertility or even my life. I yelled at God. I didn't want another trial, particularly not this one. I felt like he had capriciously sent another devastation my way.

In retrospect, I learned so much about the Lord in the midst of that terrible trial. (I even had three healthy children after the ectopic pregnancy.) I realized that God was big enough to handle my anger and honesty. I grew in empathy toward anyone who had lost a child. I realized I could handle more than I thought I was capable of, all with God's strength.

I also learned that God does allow for circumstances that seem like more than we can endure. I understood that I live in a fallen world with sin and death reigning. And like Job, I found out that God is sovereign, but he doesn't always conform to my wishes. Through all that,

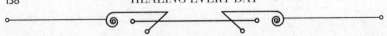

I followed the pattern of Romans 5:3-5—God granted me the ability to endure.

I don't want to repeat the pain of the past or relive my trials. Nor would I wish them on anyone. But I am grateful for the maturity God has wrought in the midst of bewildering circumstances. You may not believe in God's goodness in the middle of your current anguish, but as sure as dawn, he will carry you through, create the quality of endurance within you, and leave you with hope.

Jesus, I don't like trials. They seem to be heaped upon me. I don't understand why you don't agree with my desire to live a pain-free life. But here I am, hurting. Please help me gain a new perspective on what all this is about. I do want to endure. I long for hope. I need to know you are with me in the midst of my tears. Please be present with me today, Jesus. Amen.

Day Sixty-Five

*Overwhelming victory is ours through Christ, who loved
us. And I am convinced that nothing can ever separate us
from God's love. Neither death nor life, neither angels nor
demons, neither our fears for today nor our worries about
tomorrow—not even the powers of hell can separate us from
God's love. No power in the sky above or in the earth below—
indeed, nothing in all creation will ever be able to separate us
from the love of God that is revealed in Christ Jesus our Lord.*

ROMANS 8:37-39

Today's Scripture passage is a reminder that you are loved. Not
merely liked or tolerated or marginally accepted, but outrageously
loved. Settle into that truth a moment. The God of the universe created
you. He endowed you with worth and dignity as his image bearer. He
made a way for you to be in relationship with him through his Son's
sacrifice on the cross. This is a solid truth, one that cannot be shaken.
Nothing you do or say will ever be able to rip that truth away from you.

Because you've experienced trauma and pain in the past, you may
wonder about God's love. That's normal. But your wavering belief
doesn't negate his love. Trials don't trump God's affection for you. He
walks with you in the midst of them.

Today's passage reminds you that you *will* trek through trials like
stress, the threat of death (health issues), spiritual attack, anxiety, and
evil. Even if all these struggles are heaped upon you, the truth remains:
You are loved. To cling to that belief is what faith means. Sometimes
we tenaciously cling to his love with courage; other times, we're barely
hanging on.

Perhaps today is one of those hanging-on days. If that's the case, read
and then reread today's verses. Let them soak into you. Jesus has already

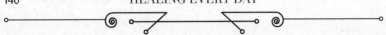

revealed his love. It's a historical fact, evidenced by his life, death, and resurrection. You cannot undo what he has done. And because he has done such powerful work on your behalf, you can rest in knowing his love will not shift. Why? Because it's not dependent on you; it's dependent on his dependability.

Jesus, thank you for your love. It's necessary. It's my breath today, my reason for continuing. There have been times when I've doubted your love. Circumstances have marred my perception of your goodness. Today, would you show me afresh that you love me? I choose to believe in the truth of your love, the finality of your work on the cross on my behalf. Amen.

Day Sixty-Six

Remember, dear brothers and sisters, that few of you were wise in the world's eyes or powerful or wealthy when God called you. Instead, God chose things the world considers foolish in order to shame those who think they are wise. And he chose things that are powerless to shame those who are powerful. God chose things despised by the world, things counted as nothing at all, and used them to bring to nothing what the world considers important. As a result, no one can ever boast in the presence of God.

1 Corinthians 1:26-29

I'm not sure when we decided that to be a Christ follower, we had to live up to certain expectations of strength, with-it-ness, or personal holiness. But that view has permeated our thinking so much that when we fail (as we are wont to do), we shrink away from Jesus and berate ourselves for not being enough for him.

But these verses push against that view. God is not looking for strong warriors. In fact, he rather likes worriers—not folks who stress about everything, per se, but people who know that without him, they can do nothing. He loves those who intrinsically recognize their need for him, who know that they are simple clay pots, and he is the splendid power within.

Here's the good news for folks who are in the middle of the healing process: We understand this truth perfectly. We know we can't heal on our own. We are well-acquainted with our weaknesses. And since we are, we no longer have to view our past as a detriment to following Jesus, but as a special gift. Because we've experienced hardship and a broken heart, we are more apt to *need* Jesus. And oh, how he loves to strengthen those whose hearts are completely his.

Yes, you may have looked foolish before. You may have experienced

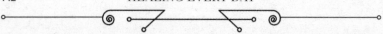

the tragedy of powerlessness. You may have been despised or utterly ignored. But all these things serve as reminders that you cannot muster up the wherewithal to impress God with your power. Your weaknesses serve to keep you humbly dependent—a beautiful place to be, where God gets the glory, and you experience his mighty strength. What a privilege!

> *Jesus, thank you that my past has served as a platform*
> *to help me understand your strength. I know I can't*
> *measure up. I know that in myself I am needy and*
> *weak. But because of that, I can run to you and*
> *experience the most incredible strength. If I could do*
> *it all, if I were stiff-necked and proud of my abilities,*
> *I would not recognize my need for you. Amen.*

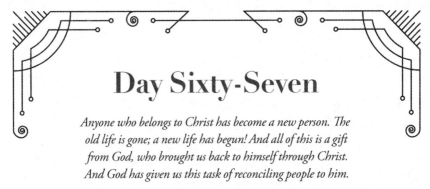

Day Sixty-Seven

Anyone who belongs to Christ has become a new person. The old life is gone; a new life has begun! And all of this is a gift from God, who brought us back to himself through Christ. And God has given us this task of reconciling people to him.

2 CORINTHIANS 5:17-18

Reconciliation is an important ministry. First, Christ reconciles us to himself through his sacrifice on the cross. And in a very real sense, he reconciles us to our own souls. Like in the story of *The Velveteen Rabbit*, we become more real in the midst of Christ's embrace. Instead of living in old patterns of behavior, we are made new—given new ways of thinking about ourselves as people who are truly reconciled.

So many of us live in the old way of thinking though—as if we are not reconciled people. Because living cautiously or pessimistically is how we processed our past life of pain, we continue to see the world that way because it's comfortable, knowable. Instead, Jesus beckons us onward and upward—away from how we used to be, toward what we can be with his help.

What would it look like if you lived reconciled? As you've been pondering the devotions from the past few days, you may have bumped up against the idea that God loves you. And perhaps that's hard to fathom. But whether you feel loved or not, the truth is that he does love you. He has already reconciled you to himself. Therefore, you can live freely in light of that truth.

How will you know that you're finally grasping that reconciled life? How will you know when you've shed the old ways of thinking in light of new, kingdom-breathed thinking? By your current relationships. You are reconciled to become a reconciler. While there may be a few relationships in your life that remain broken because of someone

else's continued bad behavior (and it's wise to separate from predatory people), the rest of your relationships will bear the mark of grace and reconnection.

Your transformed heart longs to see this: not only your relationships reconciled to you (as far as it depends on you), but also your loved ones reconciled to their God. What a privilege it is that God entrusts us with this grand ministry of reconciliation! This happens in an intersection of God's goodness, your prayers, and the surrendered life. Perhaps as you're reading this, someone who desperately needs the wholeness God provides has sprung to mind. Commit to praying for that person, asking God to bring reconciliation their way.

> *Jesus, I do want to be reconciled to myself—to be authentically me. Thank you for ushering in that type of growth through first reconciling me to yourself. Help me survey my current relationships today to see where I can be a part of reconciliation. And remind me to keep praying for those who don't yet know you. I want to be a minister of reconciliation in this broken, torn-apart world. Amen.*

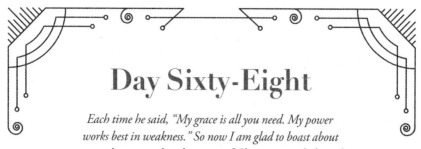

Day Sixty-Eight

Each time he said, "My grace is all you need. My power works best in weakness." So now I am glad to boast about my weaknesses, so that the power of Christ can work through me. That's why I take pleasure in my weaknesses, and in the insults, hardships, persecutions, and troubles that I suffer for Christ. For when I am weak, then I am strong.

2 Corinthians 12:9-10

Paul wanted freedom from a "thorn." It was constant, painful, and unremoved. He asked God to remove it, begged him (see 2 Corinthians 12:7-8). And yet, God answered no. Eventually, Paul began to see this "no" as part of God's loving hand in his life. The very thing that brought his deep pain made him deeply dependent on his creator.

Walking through heartache and longing for healing, we often pray prayers, asking God to please remove our thorns—broken relationships, terrible words spoken over us, autoimmune diseases, volcanic conflicts that never seem to end, financial woes, our own failures. And yet sometimes God declines our requests because he loves us. He sees beyond the horizon of our stories. He peers around the bend in the road. And he truly knows what is best for us, what will grow us, what will greatly benefit our souls.

I'm learning that when God says no, my growth is at the forefront of his mind. I am learning the hard times bring sanctification and a heart more dependent on God. In the demise of a long-term friendship, I ached, prayed, cried. But as I sit here in the midst of the pain, I realize it has caused me to pursue God more, entrust my heart to him more, and surrender afresh.

Perhaps your thorn can be a catalyst for growth too. Ask God to help you see your thorn as a recognition of your weakness, sifted

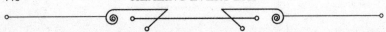

through the sovereign hands of the God who loves you and wants the best for you. When you're hurting and lack strength, instead of blaming God for his answer, thank him for his availability in the midst of the pain. Thank him for the strength he provides. Thank him that these current circumstances of loss will eventually mean a gain for your soul. Yes, insults and hardships and persecutions and troubles are thorny, but they are the very avenue God prepares for you to truly experience him.

Jesus, I don't like thorns. I would much prefer for you to take them away from me. But I want to be the kind of follower who grows closer to you every year, so I understand that you leave behind some thorns so I will learn new levels of trust in you and your paradoxical kingdom plan. Instead of fighting against this thorn, I choose to turn to you for strength and perspective today. Amen.

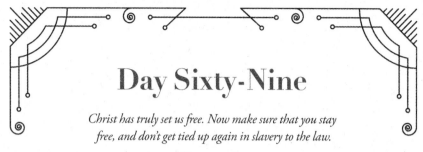

Day Sixty-Nine

Christ has truly set us free. Now make sure that you stay free, and don't get tied up again in slavery to the law.

GALATIANS 5:1

Freedom. We taste it from time to time, and we want more. Freedom from guilt. Freedom from shame. Freedom from our past. Freedom from the story we used to tell ourselves. Freedom from being overlooked. Freedom from hopelessness. Freedom from pessimism and unbelief.

Note who sets us free: Christ.

We cannot usher in our own freedom. Sure, we can make good choices in pursuing healthy relationships and enacting good boundaries around unsafe ones. We can repent of the repetitive sins that keep us in sad bondage. We can move away from legalism toward a more grace-based approach to life.

But it's Christ who brings soul freedom, an expansive view of life, a hope that makes no sense. Only Christ's sacrifice guarantees a right standing with God. Only Christ can grant the forgiveness we so desperately need—the kind of forgiveness that so woos us that we're finally able to forgive those who wronged us. It all ends and begins in Christ.

How we view Jesus will inform our pathway to healing. If we believe him anemic and irrelevant, we will not trust him on this long healing road. If we think our wholeness is entirely placed on our shoulders, we'll collapse under the weight. But if we believe Jesus is the one who heals our stories, provides the love we've always longed for, and is intimately interested in our well-being, we'll experience wholeness.

This wholeness is not granted all at once. It's a process, a journey. We aren't immediately set free from everything we struggle against. Instead, we walk it out, step by step. Jesus promises deliverance over

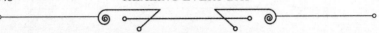

the long haul, and eventually, when we see him face-to-face, this free-dom will finally culminate. Hold on tight. I know this is a perplexingly long journey, but your Savior loves you. He does what he promises. And he will be with you, granting you freedom upon freedom as you trust in his goodness.

> *Jesus, I want to be free. Free from shame. Free from the weight of my story. Free from this unrelenting pain. But I know that you walk with me little by little, and my freedom comes in that everyday trust. My prayer is this: I want to be freer next year than I am today. I want to be more joyful, lighter, more hopeful 365 days from now. In the time between then and now, empower me to walk boldly in your freedom. Amen.*

Day Seventy

Let's not get tired of doing what is good. At just the right time we will reap a harvest of blessing if we don't give up.

GALATIANS 6:9

Giving up seems much, much easier than pushing through pain and working through the details of a traumatic past. We don't often equate this verse with the healing journey, do we? We think of persevering under trial. Or serving the poor. Or praying for a wayward friend. Or working hard at our jobs. Or serving in a ministry even when it's inconvenient.

What if "doing what is good" also means doing good to ourselves? What if God has been wooing us for years to be whole for the sake of ourselves and our loved ones? What if God is calling you to examine your present actions and how they connect to your past pain? What if healing is the holy task he asks you to tackle with perseverance?

I believe God longs for your heart to be made whole. The moment you connected with him in relationship, he began the long process of helping you heal. But there can come a time when we feel we've done enough, and we close the door to further healing. Once we have a modicum of control (which is really an illusion, but we love it nonetheless), we stop growing, examining, and pursuing.

I wish healing was a lackadaisical adventure. I have often hoped it would be passive, wishing I could sit idly by while God automatically heals me. But the journey of healing is a tandem partnership between me and the Almighty God. There is no such thing as passive healing. I have to *want* to get well. And as the journey gets long, I grow weary. My tendency is to stop.

But God promises that he will continue to heal us as we open the door to his ways. He asks us to persevere in our desire to be whole. In

that place of vulnerability, he meets us with his presence and strength. The harvest of healthy thoughts, freedom-influenced behaviors, and joy in the midst of pain will come. Do not lose heart, dear one. You are loved. You are pursued. You are worthy of healing because of God's grace. Keep at it. Press on.

Jesus, I am weary. I grow weary. I am tired of this seemingly impossible journey of healing. Why does it take so long? Why do I seem to keep struggling with the same things over and over again? I honestly can say I want to quit. But thank you that you don't quit. I choose to ask you afresh for new healing vistas. I need you. I need your encouragement today. Amen.

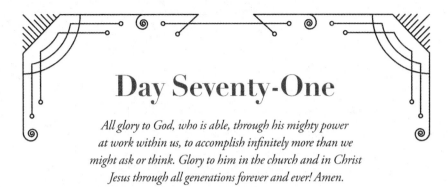

Day Seventy-One

*All glory to God, who is able, through his mighty power
at work within us, to accomplish infinitely more than we
might ask or think. Glory to him in the church and in Christ
Jesus through all generations forever and ever! Amen.*

Ephesians 3:20-21

When we become introspective about our healing, we can forget the overarching story. This story is actually not about us, nor our pain. It's about God and his glory. When I get to the point of introspection to the nth degree, I have to stop and remember this truth: I play one small part in the ever-unfolding narrative of God's spectacular (and mysterious) plan.

Even so, today's scripture offers exceptional encouragement to those of us who suffer. God's glory is the center point of all, but in the context of that, he invites us to pray audacious prayers. We can do this because of his power, which is far beyond what we can imagine.

When I was fifteen, newly a Christian, I had zero idea what God would do with me. As I struggled throughout my days to live life and try to be healthy in the aftermath of sexual abuse, neglect, and a host of other painful things, I often wondered if I would ever be whole. I prayed God would heal me, but I had no idea what that would take. Or how long.

Those tiny, uninformed prayers for health were not ignored by God. In his timing, and according to a plan I could not have invented or conceived of, he reshaped me, helped me understand some of the whys (although certainly not all), and empowered me to think differently in the aftermath of pain. I am not whole yet; that will come on the other side of eternity. But I am more whole than I was at fifteen.

Pray those bold prayers. Trust your compassionate God. Realize his

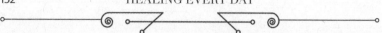

glory and story will reign in your life. You're not there yet, but you're on a journey. Whether you're wondering when you'll ever be whole or praying for health in new ways, the truth remains that God is on his glorious throne, and he will accomplish far more than you expect.

> *Jesus, sometimes I'm overwhelmed with my own need. Other times, I'm in awe of all you've already done. Help me remember that you reign through it all, through my doubts and in your power. Help me pray bold prayers today about my healing. I want to welcome you in the midst of my story. I want my story to bring you more and more glory. Amen.*

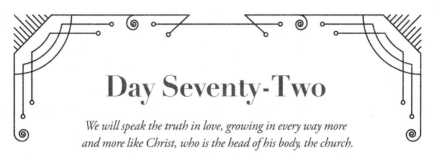

Day Seventy-Two

*We will speak the truth in love, growing in every way more
and more like Christ, who is the head of his body, the church.*

EPHESIANS 4:15

S peaking the truth is hard. Telling it with a hefty dose of love is even
harder. So often, we who have suffered have had truth flung our
way in angry words, shouts, and stern lectures. We are well aware of
our shortcomings because someone roughly shared them with us, all
veiled in the word *truth*.

So we recoil from it, fear it, shrink from it.

And when we need to tell it, we don't have a good example to draw
from. So we hide. We fail to share the truth because of fear. We don't
want to wield our words as weapons.

But Paul reminds us here that speaking the truth, if we couple it
with love, is something that ought to be normative in the Christian
community. The more we grow in this aspect of our lives, the more we
act like Jesus.

When you worry about sharing the truth (with love!), simply go
back to the Gospels and look at the way Jesus interacted with people.
He is the best example to follow, even if you've had raging people spew
truth at you in the past. Jesus didn't spew. He didn't ridicule or shame.
He asked questions. He listened. He plainly told the truth. To those
in sin, he commanded them to leave their lives of sin behind. To the
proud, he demonstrated humility while telling stories of the downfall
of proud people. And when his house became a merchant's paradise,
anger fueled his words—but he did not sin in his anger. Nor did he sin
when he expressed strong displeasure at the hypocrisy of the Pharisees.

If Jesus told the truth constantly to his disciples, friends, foes, and
followers, surely we can do the same with his Spirit within us. We can

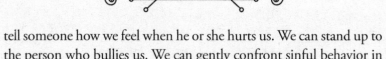

tell someone how we feel when he or she hurts us. We can stand up to the person who bullies us. We can gently confront sinful behavior in another. We can even tell the truth about ourselves, confessing our sins to Jesus and the people in our lives who are safe. The more we tell the truth with love as the backdrop, the more freedom we will experience.

Jesus, help me become one who speaks the truth in love. I want to follow your example from when you walked the earth, but I'm scared. I've had so many people belittle what I've said. I've experienced backlash when I've stood up for myself. I've sometimes coupled anger with truth. Teach me what it means to be healthy in the way I share truth. Amen.

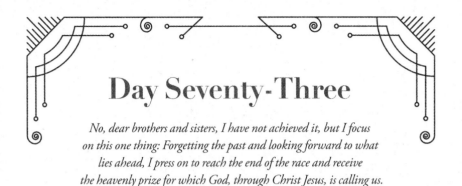

Day Seventy-Three

*No, dear brothers and sisters, I have not achieved it, but I focus
on this one thing: Forgetting the past and looking forward to what
lies ahead, I press on to reach the end of the race and receive
the heavenly prize for which God, through Christ Jesus, is calling us.*

PHILIPPIANS 3:13-14

Does this mean we completely forget about the pain in the past?
Or that we should simply never think about it again? Is God
calling us to gloss over our struggles? Taking in the whole counsel of
Scripture is important here. In order to move forward, we must look
backward to understand the dynamics of our pain.

Ignoring it will cause us to have bewildering behaviors today. For
instance, if we shove down past sexual abuse, pretending it has no bearing on our lives at present, we will be frustrated when we're triggered
by someone or something in the media.

But if we look realistically at our past pain, seek counsel (including
a doctor's advice), pray, and read Scripture in light of the past (in other
words, if we work through it), then we have the appropriate ability to
do as Paul has done—to let go of the past.

In Paul's case, he didn't forget that he used to persecute the church.
He mentions it several times throughout his letters. But he worked
through that awful period of his life. He spent 14 years outside the
public spotlight, learning what it meant to follow Jesus (see Galatians
2:1). Because of that, he could confidently tell Jesus's followers that,
although we look back to work through our past, we don't need to *stay*
there. There will come a time in your healing journey when God asks
you to move beyond the pain—just as Paul had to move beyond his
guilt and shame over persecuting the churches in order to become a
planter of churches and a church father.

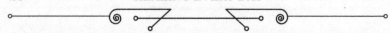

We work through our past, then let go of it in order to move forward in the ministry God has for us today. He heals our past so that we can be an agent of healing for other people's stories. But if we stay forever linked back there, we won't be able to see what God is planning for us in his kingdom. So, yes, look back there. Find healing. But don't stay in that place of brokenness. Move forward and play your part in expanding the kingdom of God, beautifully proving there is a purpose to your pain.

> *Jesus, help me walk this tightrope of my past. Am I spending too much time there? When have I shoved it down, trying to ignore it? Teach me how to let you into my past story in order to bring new healing. And give me the power to look forward to what lies ahead, to fulfill the ministry you have called me to. Thank you that my greatest pain is turning into my greatest influence. Amen.*

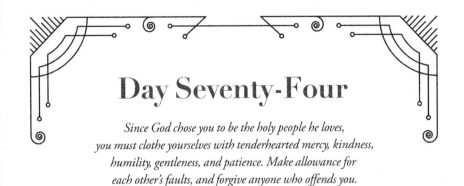

*Since God chose you to be the holy people he loves,
you must clothe yourselves with tenderhearted mercy, kindness,
humility, gentleness, and patience. Make allowance for
each other's faults, and forgive anyone who offends you.
Remember, the Lord forgave you, so you must forgive others.*

COLOSSIANS 3:12-13

Forgiving those who have harmed us is hard. Forgiving those who continue to hurt us is excruciating. But we are to forgive in the same manner Jesus forgives us, up to 70 times 7 (490 times!) and beyond (see Matthew 18:21-22). But how?

First, remember that forgiveness doesn't mean you've forgotten. Forgiveness is powerful because you remember. It's a gift you give to set free the bitterness that could fester if you held on to unforgiveness. It is a crucial part of your healing, but it's your choice. No one should force you to forgive, nor should they give you their prescribed time frame for pardon. Forgiveness is your choice, fueled by your own interaction with Jesus.

Second, remember that forgiveness recognizes the weakness of another. As we forgive others, we also realize how desperately we need forgiveness. In that tender place, we see our own sins against God and others and our own frailty. We simply cannot live perfect lives, nor can we always treat others with kindness and respect (though we may try). Because of that, in order for all of us to live in community, God has demonstrated forgiveness. It's the oxygen of the kingdom.

Forgiving someone who has abused you is tricky and painful. The perpetrator may have never asked you for forgiveness (or they may demand it after a half-baked apology). Even so, when you hold on to unforgiveness, you create a bond with that perpetrator. As long as

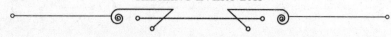

their actions hold sway over you, and you continue to want to punish them, you'll be connected. Forgiveness is the hacksaw that cuts the bond. It sets you free to live your life with joy because when you forgive, you're no longer connected to that person who hurt you, and you leave room for possible reconciliation down the road. (Reconciliation doesn't always happen, particularly when you're dealing with narcissistic or predatory people, but your forgiveness at least opens the door to the possibility *if* the other person sees their own sin.)

In short, you're most like Jesus when you forgive. He asked the Father to pardon the very people crucifying him as he was in agony on the cross. He will give you the power to do the same, no matter how hard it may be.

Jesus, I want to be like you, but I'm so hurt. How do I forgive the person who has hurt me so much? I know that by harboring bitterness, I'm connected to that person. Give me the ability to forgive. Help me remember that this one choice fuels a hundred (thousand!) more decisions to forgive in the future. I want to live in the habit of forgiveness today. Amen.

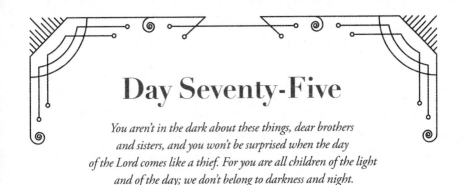

Day Seventy-Five

*You aren't in the dark about these things, dear brothers
and sisters, and you won't be surprised when the day
of the Lord comes like a thief. For you are all children of the light
and of the day; we don't belong to darkness and night.*

1 THESSALONIANS 5:4-5

G rowing up (and sometimes even now), I had a terrified view of
the dark. When the sun went down, my fear rose. On one hand,
most kids are afraid of the dark. But on another hand, my family would
have parties at night, and those get-togethers often grew from sedate to
scary in a matter of hours, punctuated by alcohol and drug abuse. The
adults in my life became most unpredictable in those situations, and I
learned how to find hiding places.

When we meet Jesus, he transfers us from one kingdom to another—
from darkness to light. Here, Paul reminds us that we are now children
of light and sunshine and daytime. The night no longer needs to hold
us in fear. And the end of our lives doesn't need to loom like a specter
in the night.

Part of moving from fear to peace is realizing the settled truth of
this transference. No matter what you've experienced, be it traumatic
or frightening, you are light. You are part of a new kingdom. You no
longer live at fear's address.

But Paul reminds us of one more thing that can also empower us as
we strive to live healed lives today: eschatological living. This is a biblical concept that simply means living in light of eternity and what is
to come. What we see here on earth (wars, famine, violence, sin run
amok, abuse) will end. There will be a time, and it will extend to forever, when God's perfect rule will shine over us all.

In that place, darkness does not exist. Jesus becomes the light that

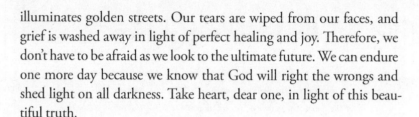

illuminates golden streets. Our tears are wiped from our faces, and grief is washed away in light of perfect healing and joy. Therefore, we don't have to be afraid as we look to the ultimate future. We can endure one more day because we know that God will right the wrongs and shed light on all darkness. Take heart, dear one, in light of this beautiful truth.

> *Jesus, help me live in light of what is to come. I know darkness has been scary—in my own life and in the lives of those I love. But I want to reorient my heart away from my fear of the dark toward the light that you give me today. It's a down payment, a promise of what will come in the new heavens and the new earth. Help me live in such a way that I'll welcome that with joy. Amen.*

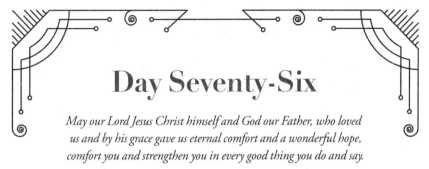

Day Seventy-Six

*May our Lord Jesus Christ himself and God our Father, who loved
us and by his grace gave us eternal comfort and a wonderful hope,
comfort you and strengthen you in every good thing you do and say.*

2 THESSALONIANS 2:16-17

Have you been down lately? Has the world pummeled your joy? Stolen your resolve? Are you walking through a relational breakup? Yes, this world can be excruciating, but there is always hope in Jesus Christ. Why? Because he loves us. He shows us grace. He gives us everything we need not merely to survive a day, but to thrive.

Eternal comfort. This is the kind of never-ending comfort that can only come from an eternal source. As we read throughout the New Testament, Jesus learned obedience through suffering, and one of the reasons he came to earth was to know what it was like for us to live on it. He understands trials. He experienced heartache, betrayal, hunger, and pain. He empathizes with us and can therefore offer us true comfort.

Wonderful hope. Hope is an elusive word. We use it casually in reference to wanting something. *I hope I get into that club. I hope he buys me that ring. I hope she says yes.* But biblical hope is more robust than simply wishing on circumstances. This hope is assured. It's rock solid. It's based on the finished work of Jesus on the cross and his subsequent resurrection. When we walk through trial upon trial, hope shines. When we feel like we're mired in the healing journey, making little progress, hope waits for us. There is hope we can rely on today, but there's also the hope that we will be delivered from trials one day, and we will experience complete healing as well—on heaven's shores.

In the meantime, these verses promise us something tangible as we wait between the now and the not yet: comfort and strength for today. Are you worried? Ask for Jesus's comfort. Are you weakened by your

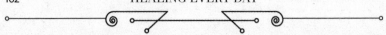

life? Ask for Jesus's strength. He is available in this moment. He waits for you to call on him. He is faithful, ready, and alive. And he loves to love you. Trust in that today.

> *Jesus, I do need comfort and hope. Especially as I consider what I've walked through on this earth and what I may face in the future. Instead of resigning myself to sadness or fear, I choose to go to you, ask for your strength, and trust that you are in control, even when my life careens into crazy places. Oh, how I need you. Thank you for solid hope. Thank you for being the God of comfort today. Amen.*

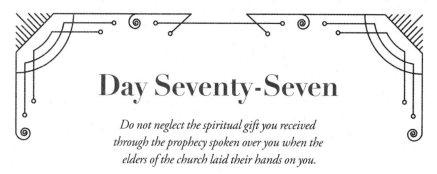

Day Seventy-Seven

Do not neglect the spiritual gift you received
through the prophecy spoken over you when the
elders of the church laid their hands on you.

1 TIMOTHY 4:14

W e all are graced with gifts. When we trusted Jesus as our Savior, he stirred up gifts within us, pathways to both find him
and help others. These gifts can beautifully serve our healing journey.

One thing I realized growing up was that I could write. Others con-
firmed this. I processed a lot of my pain in journals—the sadness over
my father's untimely death, my fear of being taken, the loneliness I
constantly faced, my worry that I'd repeat the antics of my family. This
served me well. But when I met Jesus, this gift seemed to flourish. It
moved from the written word to the spoken word.

A big part of my healing journey came when I shared my story after
I met Jesus. He gifted me to authentically weave the narrative of my life
in such a way that drew people toward me. And thankfully, those people were praying people who laid hands on me (much like today's passage refers to) and trusted God to heal me.

The gift he gave me became the means of healing. Later, when I
wrote a book, he used my own writing to heal broken parts of myself.
When I speak, a similar thing happens.

How has God gifted you? Have you considered that the gift he's
given you may be a means of healing? Do you feel more alive and connected to him when you serve others? Has your gift of administration
given you a new way of categorizing your past? When you've inter-
ceded for someone else, has God met you there as well?

Pay attention to the way God has gifted you. Look back on the
times of your life when you were operating with joy in that gift. Do

you also see healing during those times? Isn't it amazing that while God's gifts to us are, of course, for the body of Christ, they're also for us? Gifts are a deposit of heaven, an indication of God's presence in our lives, and they can be a beautiful means of healing in our own journeys. Thank him for that.

> *Jesus, wow. Thank you for giving me a gift when I met you—a unique ability that helps others but also helps me. Give me eyes to see how the gift you've given can be a part of my own healing journey. Thank you that you are the God of gifts, that you give all your children abilities that will empower them throughout life. Help me uncover the nuances of the gift you've given me today. Amen.*

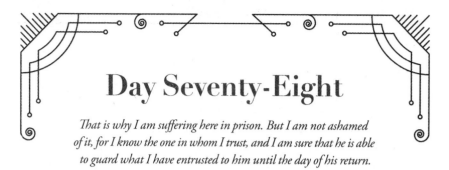

Day Seventy-Eight

That is why I am suffering here in prison. But I am not ashamed
of it, for I know the one in whom I trust, and I am sure that he is able
to guard what I have entrusted to him until the day of his return.

2 TIMOTHY 1:12

Although we don't know much of what the apostle Paul's upbringing was like, we do know he lived with regrets in terms of how he persecuted the church. He must've had wounds from others as well. Even though some of us experienced figurative prisons growing up, Paul lived in a literal prison later in life. How he endured that trial is instructive for all of us.

What did he do?

Paul acknowledged the pain he walked through. He said he suffered in the midst of his imprisonment. Paul's example helps us realize that it's okay to be honest about our current pain. There is no shame in sharing how hard our lives are in this moment. There's nothing wrong with weeping over the past either. When we're honest, we agree with God about our situation, and we invite others to share the burden as well.

Paul was not ashamed of the pain. He realized the universal truth that pain hurts. Imprisonment is confining. It's simply the reality. He didn't ask to be imprisoned any more than we ask to be betrayed. So there's no shame in acknowledging that someone hurt us.

Paul knew Jesus. In the midst of his imprisonment, his goal was to know Jesus more and more. He didn't allow chains to prevent him from worshipping or learning or encountering Christ. His prison cell was no excuse. Paul learned the art of thriving where he was, despite his confinement.

Paul trusted Jesus. He knew him to be faithful. Even if Paul experienced prison, nothing could imprison the gospel (see 2 Timothy 2:9).

It would progress gloriously. All that Paul accomplished was never wasted. In fact, one could argue that the gospel spread widely because of it. When we look back on our prisons, times in our lives when we felt helpless or confined by someone else's decisions, we, too, can find comfort in knowing that God's purposes for our lives cannot and will not be thwarted by difficult circumstances. What hope we have in him!

> *Jesus, thank you that nothing can prevent your*
> *purposes for my life from coming to fruition. Even*
> *when others hurt me, I can trust you. I can be utterly*
> *honest with you about the pain I've experienced*
> *or will experience. Keep me close to you in hard*
> *times. I pray I would learn how to worship you from*
> *whatever prison cell in which I find myself. Amen.*

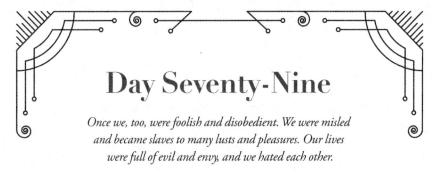

Day Seventy-Nine

*Once we, too, were foolish and disobedient. We were misled
and became slaves to many lusts and pleasures. Our lives
were full of evil and envy, and we hated each other.*

Titus 3:3

When you're discouraged about your journey, it's good to look back on the progress you've made. Here, Paul reflects on his life and fellow believers' lives before Christ—and they were full of mayhem. Foolishness. Disobedience. Enslavement. Hatred.

What do you see in your past? There are two ways we can look at it: what was done to us, and the way we responded to how others treated us.

When we consider our stories, it's somewhat easier to recount all the ways others have hurt us. We're living in the repercussions of other people's decisions after all. While it's healthy to acknowledge the pain of what others put us through, it's also important to move beyond their actions by living a renewed life. Yes, that pain is legitimate, but because of what Jesus has done by intersecting our lives, he is now in the process of redeeming those situations for our good and his glory.

What's harder to do when we look back is to honestly recount our own decisions and actions before Christ. In other words, how did we respond to life? What were our sinful choices? How did we think? What did we do that brought dishonor upon ourselves and others? While it may be easy to rattle off the sins that others committed against us, it's harder to agree that we, too, have made sinful choices. Even harder: We have also been a part of someone else's past negative story by the way we treated them.

But simply acknowledging past hurt (whether inflicted by others or something you did) isn't the point of today's reading. The beauty

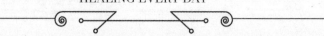

of looking back is to see the progress Jesus has wrought in you since those moments. What has he done in your life? How has he healed you from past pain? How has he intersected your choices, thoughts, and actions? Next time you're discouraged about the length and breadth of the healing journey, remember where you came from. Look at how faithful Jesus has been. You are no longer foolish, disobedient, misled, enslaved, evil, envious, or hateful. You have been delivered, and you will continue to be healed and delivered. There is joy in knowing that.

Jesus, thank you for loving me. Thank you for walking with me on this long journey of healing. As I look back, I see how others have hurt me and how I've hurt others. And I'm grateful you have redeemed those moments and have chosen to heal me and work miracles in me. Because of you, I have walked a long journey; I've come a long way. I praise you today, living in utter gratitude because of all you've done. Amen.

Day Eighty

I always thank my God when I pray for you, Philemon.

PHILEMON 4

What a beautiful picture of deep friendship—a sweet relationship connected by prayer. These are the kinds of friends we need as we navigate the healing path. I've mentioned before that healing cannot occur in isolation. As I write this, my husband's been away for several days on business, and I can sense my mind getting tied up because I have nowhere for my (many!) words to go. He helps untangle me.

Friends are our greatest allies on this pursuit of wholeness. They gently correct, listen to our hearts, sit quietly alongside us while we grieve, speak the truth to us in critical times, don't settle for our complacency, and pray for us in all circumstances. They untangle us.

One side effect of our past pain, though, can be the evisceration of our existing friendships. We become so hurt by life and others that we protect ourselves by erecting razor-wire walls around our hearts. So, when we're triggered by the past or can't seem to get out of bed, we look at our phones and wonder who would even want to hear from us. Our isolation makes it hard for us to reenter friendships we've pushed away. And in that place, our loneliness compounds our pain, creating a cycle (more like a cyclone!) of sadness.

Friends are God's sweet gift to us. Yes, it may be true that some of our friends didn't act becomingly in the past. Some may have gossiped about us or betrayed us. But it's important we don't throw out all friendships because some were bad. Today you have the opportunity to reach out to someone—perhaps an existing friend, a past friend, or a potential friend. Simply ask this question: "How can I pray for you today?" Prayer opens up a relationship in unique ways. It cuts through

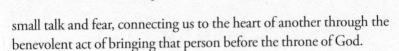

small talk and fear, connecting us to the heart of another through the benevolent act of bringing that person before the throne of God.

If you're struggling with loneliness today, and you realize that you need friends on your healing journey, pray this: *Jesus, please send me one friend. Help me be alert to whom that might be.* Then be open to whomever God brings your way. You may be happily confounded, since new friends often come in surprising packages.

Jesus, I want to be a praying friend for someone who is hurting. I want to be a part of their healing story. I also recognize my need for others as I pursue wholeness. Would you please send me a friend? Instead of pushing others away in fear, help me embrace one person in faith, trusting that you will be in the midst of our friendship. I vow to take it slowly and naturally, and as I do, please help me become a friend who prays for friends. Amen.

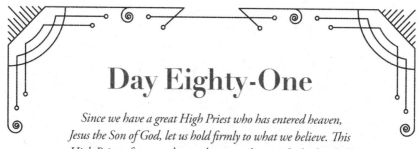

Day Eighty-One

*Since we have a great High Priest who has entered heaven,
Jesus the Son of God, let us hold firmly to what we believe. This
High Priest of ours understands our weaknesses, for he faced all
of the same testings we do, yet he did not sin. So let us come boldly
to the throne of our gracious God. There we will receive
his mercy, and we will find grace to help us when we need it most.*

HEBREWS 4:14-16

Y ou are not alone.

You are not the only one who has suffered at the hands of others.
You are understood.

Why? Jesus has undergone the same types of trials and testing as we
have. When he walked this earth, he experienced betrayal, relational
discord, abuse, nakedness, disloyalty, verbal harassment, and abandonment. And because he endured all this without sinning once, he aptly
knows how to help us when we experience similar heartache.

These verses speak of boldness. They connote the audacity of a
king's son running through the throne room, past dignitaries and officials, to scamper onto the king's lap. That is the kind of boldness we
can have when we approach the throne of grace for help. No shrinking back. No pauses and stutters. Just a welcoming embrace because
of our relationship.

Jesus's life, death, and resurrection provide us with this kind of
audacious boldness. His empathy further beckons us. Not only is he
our creator, but he powerfully understands all that we've faced. Because
of that, he best knows how to help us.

You may feel far from him today. You may be angry that he allowed
such pain in your life. But remember this: God the Father allowed
his Son to endure hatred and death—for your sake. He understands

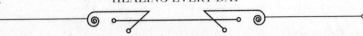

grief and pain. And in this moment, right here as you read these words black and white on the page, you can reconnect with the one who loves you that much—who sacrificed for you and gave his life for your sake, enduring the sinful behavior of others. What beautiful news! So go ahead: Run through the throne room and settle into the embrace of the God who loves you.

> *Jesus, thank you. How can I thank you enough for walking on this dusty earth, experiencing heartache and undeniable pain? Thank you that I don't have to shrink back from asking for your help or presence. Today, I choose to run to you, to accept your embrace, to receive your healing love. Amen.*

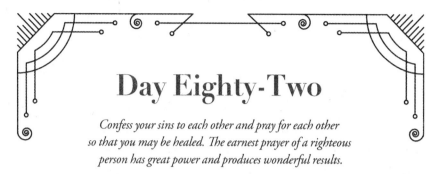

Day Eighty-Two

*Confess your sins to each other and pray for each other
so that you may be healed. The earnest prayer of a righteous
person has great power and produces wonderful results.*

JAMES 5:16

When we think of the healing journey, we often contemplate the sins others have committed against us. If we focus on them for too long, our hearts become embittered and our outlook fades to suspicion. If bitterness takes over, it serves as the lens in which we view the entire world. Everyone is out to get us. The world is bleak and wants to steal from us. Farther down this path, we find ourselves isolated and far from God.

If that describes you, first know you are not alone. And you are entirely normal. When someone sins against us, particularly in a predatory way over years and years, your shrinking away serves as a protective countermeasure. But eventually, when you are free from the person who hurt you, you need to reengage in the world, or bitterness will take over and poison your heart.

That's where the power of confession enters. It's one thing to confess your bitterness and wrath in the quiet of your bedroom. It's quite another to admit it openly to a safe person in a circle of prayer. When you let out your pain in the company of another, it loses its power over you. Community is God's avenue to bring you healing, and confession is the fuel to see that happen.

Maybe you're not bitter. Maybe you're simply hurting over someone else's antics toward you, or you're frustrated that God doesn't seem to be answering your prayers. Even in those situations, it's healthy to confess what you're feeling in the presence of another. When you do

that, you give someone else the privilege of bearing your burden. When you wall yourself off, you take away that privilege.

Whether you're confessing your own sin of bitterness or wrangling over the pain of someone else's sin against you, find a trusted person with whom you can process your pain. You'll be surprised at how free you'll feel afterward. Why? Because we were not designed to walk the Christian life alone.

Jesus, if I still have bitterness in my heart or unforgiveness, will you reveal that to me? I want to be set free from being jaded and suspicious. And Lord? I'm still hurting from what those folks did to me so long ago. I want to be free of that pain too. Would you show me someone I can process this with in prayer? Amen.

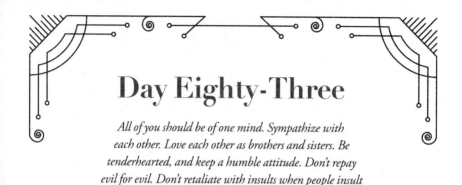

Day Eighty-Three

*All of you should be of one mind. Sympathize with
each other. Love each other as brothers and sisters. Be
tenderhearted, and keep a humble attitude. Don't repay
evil for evil. Don't retaliate with insults when people insult
you. Instead, pay them back with a blessing. That is what
God has called you to do, and he will grant you his blessing.*

1 Peter 3:8-9

What powerful verses for those who struggle with a painful past!
Peter shows us a relational blueprint as to how we should live
in this world. And as we read through what he writes, it also serves as
a measuring stick of our growth.

First, Peter assumes his readers are in community. And once we're
in that safe space of community, he encourages us to be of one mind.
That doesn't necessarily mean conformity but instead speaks to our
posture of love. We should be of one mind in our desire to outdo each
other as we love.

Peter further explains what this one mind should look like: sympathy, familial love, tenderheartedness, and humility. The presence
of those four qualities alone would cause everyone to flock to a faith
community! Who doesn't need quiet sympathy, the love of a non-
dysfunctional family, kind people, and friends who don't flaunt their
power?

Peter also addresses what an unsafe community would look like.
He gives us a glimpse of how a spiritually abusive church or ministry might appear. An unsafe spiritual community retaliates, tit for tat.
It's the kind of gathering where we constantly fear we'll be found out
for something we didn't even do, harboring an atmosphere of witch-
hunting and suspicion. Instead of blessing one another, folks make

snide comments, unfounded judgmental statements, and harsh criticisms. Unfortunately, because many of us have grown up in homes like this, we can gravitate to churches with similar mannerisms and dysfunction, which reinjures us, causing us to run a million miles away from Jesus.

Does that mean people in a safe community don't sin? Of course not. See what Peter encourages us to do: Pay back people who insult you with a blessing. The difference between a safe community full of sinners and an unsafe, spiritually abusive environment is wide. In one, you can be yourself, ask forgiveness, and grant the same. In the other, you feel like you are wrong just for being yourself, and you constantly feel insecure. Take a good look at your community today and see if your spiritual environment is safe or predatory.[2]

Jesus, help me discern if my place of worship is safe or not. In the meantime, teach me again to be the kind of community member who is humble, teachable, open, kindhearted, and forgiving. Open my eyes to what others can teach me about you. And keep me alert to those who may undermine my sense of security in you. Amen.

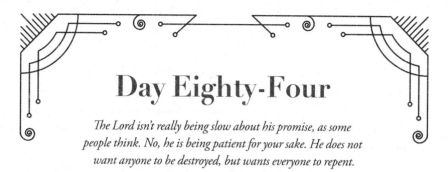

Day Eighty-Four

The Lord isn't really being slow about his promise, as some people think. No, he is being patient for your sake. He does not want anyone to be destroyed, but wants everyone to repent.

2 PETER 3:9

In our lifetimes, God seems slow. We see things through our limited lenses, wondering why God takes so long to answer our cries. We forget that God holds eternity in his hands. He also works in and through every human's story in the midst of his grand story. Only God can do such a timely and beautiful weaving.

God's "slowness" is attributed to his affection for his people. He longs for all to come to know him. He longs to see as many as possible repent. Why? Because we were created to be in relationship with him, and when we are not, our hearts wither. Abundant life comes from being connected to the one who not only fashioned us in our mother's womb, but also created us for relationship with him.

As you seek healing, your heart enlarges to conform to God's. You, too, will long to see others come to know him as you have. This also extends to the people in your past who have hurt you. At first, you may have prayed imprecatory prayers (prayers that God would enact justice and vengeance upon your "enemy"). As God healed past wounds, you may have made the important decision to release the person from your anger by forgiving them. Your imprecatory prayer might have morphed to: *Please save the person who hurt me so they can see what they've done and finally apologize.* And as you grew closer to Jesus, who pardoned the very people who crucified him, your prayer grew more intense. *Oh Lord, help this person to finally understand your love. Even if they never apologize to me.*

Wherever you are on this prayer quest, the truth remains: God

still longs for your "enemy" to know him. And he may be slow about answering your prayers, not only because of his timing, but in order to teach you to deepen your requests, moving away from a focus on you and toward a desire for the well-being of the one who harmed you. This is a difficult journey, but as you pray for your enemies this way, you'll find your heart more in tune with the God who desires that none would perish.

> *Jesus, teach me how to pray for those who have hurt me. I confess that there have been times when I'd rather have had you deal justly with them. But I want to also become a person who longs to see them repent and find your love. Empower me to release those who have hurt me into your hands. Amen.*

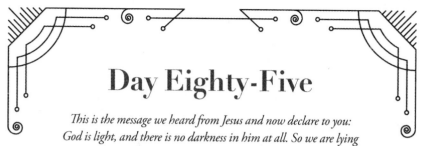

Day Eighty-Five

This is the message we heard from Jesus and now declare to you:
God is light, and there is no darkness in him at all. So we are lying
if we say we have fellowship with God but go on living in spiritual
darkness; we are not practicing the truth. But if we are living in
the light, as God is in the light, then we have fellowship with each
other, and the blood of Jesus, his Son, cleanses us from all sin.

1 JOHN 1:5-7

Often when we look at our past, we see darkness. Especially if we've experienced trauma. For a long period of time, I could only recollect the dark things that happened to me growing up. I honestly believed only bad things occurred. But an interesting thing happened after I went through further counseling in my thirties—good memories surfaced. Light broke through.

If you're encountering something similar, where you cannot recall anything light, hang in there. One way you'll know you've experienced more healing is if you begin to recall snippets of light in the midst of your dark story. If you continue to see only dark, begin to ask God to reveal little snapshots of good.

Today's passage addresses darkness as it relates to sin, and this includes sin perpetrated against you. The good news is that as a Christ follower, light will inevitably break through. While there are no guarantees that you'll have fellowship with those who have harmed you, you can do everything you can on your part to make a way for that to happen by choosing to forgive. (Remember, though, that other people can choose darkness over the long haul, and reconciliation may not be possible.)

You also have the freedom today to repent (or turn away from) sin that lurks in your heart. Sometimes, we choose sinful patterns as

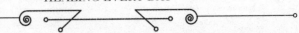

a result of abuse. For instance, we can push away good relationships because we're living in fear of being harmed again. We can turn to substances rather than our Savior. We may run to promiscuity in search of the love we didn't experience as children. The good news is that Jesus is waiting here for you, in your place of brokenness—whether it be from other people's sins or your own. Freedom is on your threshold, friend. Find a safe person, confess your hurt and sin, and experience new emancipation today.

> *Jesus, help me remember snapshots of sunlight in my past story. Would you resurrect those memories for me? And give me the courage today to once again forgive those who hurt me. I repent, too, of what I've done that has displeased you. Instead of turning to you, I chose to pursue other ways of finding relief. Forgive me. I want to experience your nearness today. Amen.*

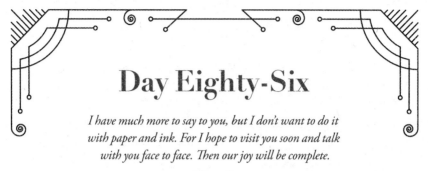

Day Eighty-Six

*I have much more to say to you, but I don't want to do it
with paper and ink. For I hope to visit you soon and talk
with you face to face. Then our joy will be complete.*

2 JOHN 12

In a world of pixels and screens, we've lost the beauty of face-to-face interaction with people. Even John faced this dilemma two millennia ago. He knew the limitations of words written on a page and preferred to have fellowship with people in person, where fewer misunderstandings could erupt.

I receive countless emails from people who are lonely. Achingly so. Some threaten harm to themselves. Others write of suicide. Of course, in those moments, I send as much help as I can. But inevitably, I have to ask: "Do you have any in-person friends? Are you consistently gathering with a community of believers?" Often the answer is no.

I know it's a risk to entrust your heart to someone else, particularly if others have deeply wounded you in the past. But you will not experience the help you need through the internet. You will not feel the actual embrace of Jesus behind a screen. You need people. And the body of Christ needs you.

I wish I could leap through this book and embrace you. I wish we could sit for lunch and unpack your story. I would pray with you, and we would share stories and tears. My prayer for you as you walk through this devotional healing journey is this: that you would find safe people who will love you well, pray daring prayers on your behalf, and bring you a casserole when you're mourning. Isolation breeds loneliness and despair. Community, when it's safe, ushers in healing.

If you've reached out to new people (again) and experienced heartache, perhaps it's time to seek some counseling to discern why you

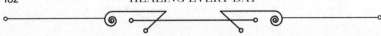

choose these kinds of relationships,[3] or maybe you should read a book about safe relationships.[4] If you continue to entrust your heart to people who eviscerate it, you'll find yourself spiraling away from others, and your healing journey will be relegated to isolation again. My prayer for you is that you'll find good, healthy friendships—face-to-face relationships that will bless and encourage you on your healing journey.

Jesus, I admit that it's easier to isolate myself behind a screen. In real life, folks have hurt me beyond recognition, and I'm terrified to try reaching out again. Teach me what it means to find safe people to interact with. Show me someone I can begin to trust. I am only capable of small steps toward a relationship like that, but I am willing to try with your help. Amen.

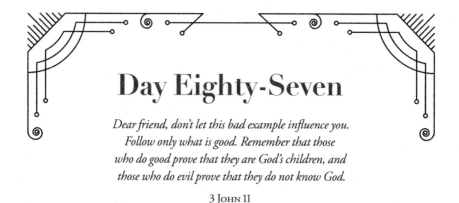

Day Eighty-Seven

Dear friend, don't let this bad example influence you.
Follow only what is good. Remember that those
who do good prove that they are God's children, and
those who do evil prove that they do not know God.

3 John 11

When you've been injured in a faith community, healing can feel impossible. The very people who should have protected you turned out to be wolves in sheep's clothing. We can rightly blame folks like that for their behavior, but then wrongly project their actions onto God, cutting ourselves off from the very real help he provides. In other words, we throw out God because of the actions of those who say they follow him.

But John reminds us of an important truth in today's verse: Actions speak louder than faith words. If an eloquent person says persuasive things about God, it doesn't mean he is a Christ follower. It simply means he can use his words in a way that makes him look like a believer. It will be his (or her) actions that verify faith.

How incredibly confusing it is when people who we think are sheep start tearing into us like ravenous wolves, all the while spewing the language of Christianity. If this has happened to you, go through the Gospels and the Epistles and do a study on wolves, false teachers, and false prophets. Harsh words of criticism are leveled at pretenders like these. Things will not end well for them.

Untangling abuse within the church is excruciating. If this has happened to you, please seek the aid of a wise counselor, particularly one who specializes in dealing with spiritual abuse. The confusion and anger you must feel makes sense. And you're not wrong to be cautious

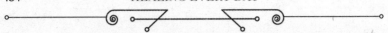

in trusting Christians who enter your life. It will take some time to work through the abuse that happened in a Christian context.

John reminds us that those who follow Christ do deeds that reflect him. Their good hearts (that have gone through a radical transformation because of Christ) can't help but produce good fruit. Those who masquerade as Christians but whose hearts are far from Christ cannot help but produce bad fruit. The problem comes when words and actions collide (good words, bad actions). I believe this is why Jesus says, "If you cause one of these little ones who trusts in me to fall into sin, it would be better for you to have a large millstone tied around your neck and be drowned in the depths of the sea" (Matthew 18:6).

Jesus, help me discern the hearts of the folks in my life, particularly those who say Christian words but act unbecomingly in the next instant. Enable me to untangle abuse within the church and see it for what it is: wolves in sheep's clothing enacting havoc within a congregation. I want to heal from this. I need to. Give me your perspective. Heal my broken heart. Amen.

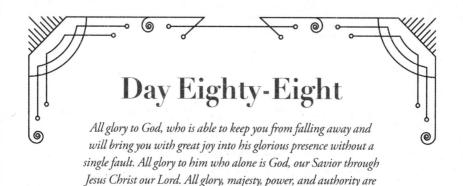

Day Eighty-Eight

All glory to God, who is able to keep you from falling away and will bring you with great joy into his glorious presence without a single fault. All glory to him who alone is God, our Savior through Jesus Christ our Lord. All glory, majesty, power, and authority are his before all time, and in the present, and beyond all time! Amen.

JUDE 24-25

As we're nearing the end of our time together in this devotional, what a beautiful passage to reflect upon! I pray these verses over your life to the God who keeps you close, who empowers you with joy. No matter where you are in your healing journey, you can be assured of this: Jesus is alive and well. He is worthy of your worship. And the more you simply sit in a place of awe toward him, the more you'll experience his healing presence.

You may feel like you're unable. But God is able.

You may feel like falling away, giving up, letting go of your faith. The journey's been so long, and while little victories have come, they have been hard won. Weariness has settled in on your journey toward wholeness. In these times of brokenness, remember the faithfulness of the one who loves you. He will not leave you. He will not turn his back on you. He will be with you always, to the end of the age. He keeps his promises, even when your resolve has dissolved.

What a gift we have in Jesus—the Savior who understands our weaknesses, experienced our heartache on the deepest level known to humankind, and took our infirmities upon his shoulders. What he did on the cross was similar to him seeing you frozen by fear in front of a barreling train, pushing you away, and receiving the full weight of steel and gears and forward momentum upon himself. He saved your life by sacrificing his.

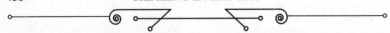

He who performed such intentional heroism is the one who formed you, loves you, and pursues your heart. He, like you, has experienced the traumatic pain of life on this earth, and he best knows how to shoulder your questions, triggers, hurts, and fear. Oh, how he loves you! He is glory, majesty, power, and authority personified. He is everything you need, the best friend you can find. Though lofty and exalted, he understands your struggle on earth. And he invites you into relationship with him—the kind of friendship that will stick with you forever. He has also given you the Holy Spirit, a constant, comforting companion who will never leave you. If that's not enough, he inaugurated a clean slate for you—grace upon grace, forgiveness, and joy.

Jesus, I need you. I love you. I am in awe of all you've done. Forgive me for running away from you in my hurt. I realize now that you empathize with my pain and you're inviting me to walk alongside you on this healing journey. It's been so hard. I've grown weary. But I understand now that I desperately need you. Be close. Revive my heart, dear Jesus. Amen.

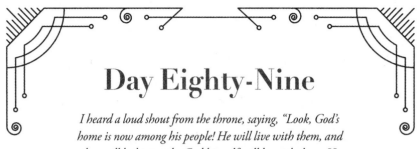

Day Eighty-Nine

I heard a loud shout from the throne, saying, "Look, God's home is now among his people! He will live with them, and they will be his people. God himself will be with them. He will wipe every tear from their eyes, and there will be no more death or sorrow or crying or pain. All these things are gone forever." And the one sitting on the throne said, "Look, I am making everything new!" And then he said to me, "Write this down, for what I tell you is trustworthy and true."

REVELATION 21:3-5

S o many tears. I look back on my life and wonder how many gallons, ponds, lakes, oceans I've cried over my past. But in this beautiful passage, we see the end of all this mourning, a holy wiping away of the pain slate. No more death. No more sorrow. No more crying. No more pain. These foes will be gone forever, evaporating like a mist upon the morning.

When you're at your lowest, read this reminder in Revelation 21. Today is not all there is. The sorrow you're trudging through matters. It counts for something. Your faithfulness in the messy middle of life will be rewarded. Every unseen obedience is chronicled by the one who loves you, who is *for* you. Not only will the new heavens and the new earth hold reward for work done on his behalf, but it will also be a place of tranquility and utter joy.

I don't know how the Lord will do this. Does he erase our memories of pain? Or give us a grander view of his incomprehensible (at least on earth) plan? Will we suddenly understand the why of our past in light of the joy of that new day? Or will it be that when our bodies are resurrected, our minds are at peace, and we're finally reunited with the one

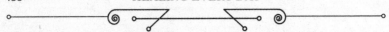

who loves us, we will no longer need any other source of love? Whatever the case, we'll be content, set free, and the most alive we've ever been.

I know you've walked a painful journey. I'm sure you still battle sleepless nights, times of anger and questioning, broken stories, and painful relationships. But this wrestling is the middle of your narrative, not the end. The end will be glorious. It will make sense. The denouement of your story will set all things aright. In the meantime, press on. Persevere. Trust the one who loves you so deeply. Believe that he will bring you closer and closer to wholeness on this earth, but he'll complete that work beautifully on the other side.

> *Jesus, help me persevere when my relationships are suffering here on earth. Keep me close to you as I face my past, grieve what's been lost, and hope for healing. I don't want to give up. I want to trust you here on earth. But on those days when my life feels dark and bleak, remind me of this promise: You will make everything right, and my tears will be wiped away. Amen.*

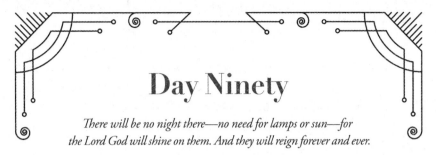

Day Ninety

There will be no night there—no need for lamps or sun—for the Lord God will shine on them. And they will reign forever and ever.

REVELATION 22:5

From darkness to light—this is the promise Jesus gives those who follow him. My prayer is that this healing-themed devotional has brought you on a journey away from darkness and varying shades of gray into a joyful beckoning of light.

Yes, you've experienced heartache. That is true. Yes, you've walked through deep and scary forests with foes aplenty. Yes, you've endured much at the hands of others bent on destroying and de-storying you. But yes, you will get through this. Yes, you will experience more and more healing. Yes, you are not merely the product of your past. Yes, you're a child of the God who loves to redeem and rewrite stories.

Your past is a painful gift. It brought you to the feet of Jesus. Because of the pain, you intrinsically knew your need for him. You began a journey of healing the moment your scared hand slipped into his scarred one.

Jesus is your wounded healer. He walked where you walked, experiencing every human heartache. He understands. And he loves you too much to let you remain enslaved to your past. No longer encaged by the voices of the past, you are now gloriously uncaged to sing the songs he put in your heart to sing.

Keep holding his hand. Keep fleeing the cage of your past. Keep singing.

There will come a day on the other side of eternity when all of it will make sense, when the pain will fade into oblivion, and you'll be reunited with the one who shepherded you through many agonies and disappointments.

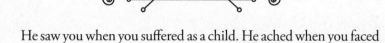

He saw you when you suffered as a child. He ached when you faced heartache as a teen. He knows your entire story—childhood, adolescence, adulthood—and he seeks to redeem it even today.

I can leave you with no other gift except the greatest of all: Jesus. He loves you. He "gets" you. He will heal you. He will shine upon you—his child of light.

> *Jesus, thank you for walking me through this journey of healing. Thank you for seeing me as a child, teen, and adult, empowering me to understand your love along the way. I know I have a long pathway in front of me, but this is my prayer: Would you redeem my story? Would you uncage me so I can sing? I want to make sense of the past pain by sharing your goodness with others. Heal me so I can be an agent of healing in this hurting world. Amen.*

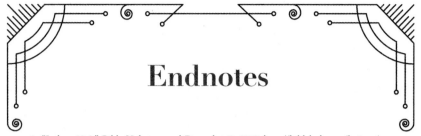

Endnotes

1. "Joshua 23:8," Bible Hub, accessed December 7, 2017, http://biblehub.com/lexicon/joshua/23-8.htm.

2. For a more robust list of qualities in a spiritually abusive church, see http://www.marydemuth.com/spiritual-abuse-10-ways-to-spot-it/

3. Read my book *The Seven Deadly Friendships* (Harvest House, 2018) for a definition of unsafe relationships and how to move beyond them.

4. I recommend you read *Safe People: How to Find Relationships That Are Good for You and Avoid Those That Aren't* (Zondervan, 2016) by Dr. Henry Cloud and Dr. John Townsend.

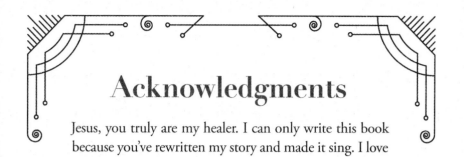

Acknowledgments

Jesus, you truly are my healer. I can only write this book because you've rewritten my story and made it sing. I love you.

Thank you to the countless people who have played a crucial role in my healing journey through Young Life and college, church and prayer groups, friendships and counselors, and my husband, Patrick, who has been like a rock for me on the shifting sands of healing.

As well, I'm grateful for the Writing Prayer Circle that faithfully prays for me every two weeks—all of which are faithful friends. Thank you, Kathi, Sandi, Holly, Renee, Caroline, Cheramy, Jeanne, D'Ann, Darren, Dorian, Erin, Helen, Katy G., Katy R., Anita, Diane, Cyndi, Leslie, Liz, Rebecca, Sarah, Tim, Tina, Nicole, Tosca, TJ, Patrick, Jody, Susan, Becky, Dena, Carol, Susie, Christy, Alice, Randy, Paul, Jan, Thomas, Judy, Aldyth, Sue, Brandilyn, Lisa, Richard, Michele, Yanci, Cristin, Roy, Michelle, Ocieanna, Denise, Heidi, Kristin, Sarah, Phyllis, Emilie, Lea Ann, Boz, Patricia, Anna, Kendra, Gina, Ralph, Sophie, Anna, Jodie, Hope, Ellen, Lacy, Tracy, Susie May, Becky, Paula, John, Julie, Dusty, Tabea, Jessica, Cheri, Shelley, Elain, Ally, and Amy. Any success in terms of the kingdom comes on the shoulders of your prayers.

Thank you to David and Sarah VanDiest who not only empower my career, but get on their knees and pray.

Thank you, Harvest House, for believing in the need for this book. I'm grateful for Bob Hawkins, Jr. and his heart to see others healed. Thank you, Kathleen Kerr and Amber

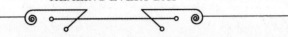

Holcomb, for keeping my voice and catching my messes. Sherry Slopianka, thank you for practically jumping up and down for my books. Thanks Jessica Ballestrazze for marketing well, and Christianne Debysingh for your expertise. Thank you Ken Lorenz for tirelessly getting my books into people's hands. Betty Fletcher, thanks for your eagle eye and keeping the logistics of book creation running smoothly. Thanks, too, to Emily Weigel Design for the book's cover—I love the aesthetic you've created.

Thank you to my church home, Lake Pointe Church, in Rockwall, Texas. You've believed in me, empowered my message, and prayed for me many years.

To Patrick, I appreciate your ability to endure with me over these long years of healing. And Sophie, Aidan, and Julia: you're precisely the reasons I pursued healing in the first place. I wanted you to have a safe, joyful, grace-filled home.

About the Author

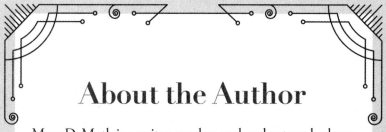

Mary DeMuth is a writer, speaker, and podcaster who loves to help people live re-storied lives. Author of more than 35 books, including Christian living titles, Southern fiction, and her latest devotional entitled *Jesus Every Day*, Mary speaks around the country and the world. She is the wife of Patrick and the mom of three adult children. Find out more at MaryDeMuth.com.

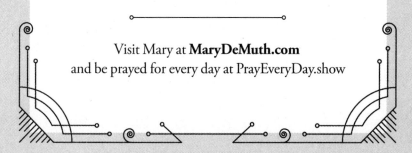

Visit Mary at **MaryDeMuth.com**
and be prayed for every day at PrayEveryDay.show

More from
Mary DeMuth

Jesus Every Day

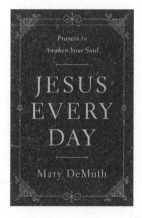

Passionate author and speaker Mary DeMuth puts into writing the hopes, worries, desires, needs, and uncertainties of everyday life so you can release them to your Savior.

With 365 daily prayers, you'll find renewed inspiration as you come before the Lord.

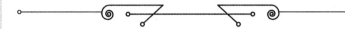

The Seven Deadly Friendships

There's something wrong with your friendship, but you can't figure out why. Is everything in your head? Unfortunately, toxic friendships happen to everyone, but we seldom identify the underlying issues while we battle confusion or the friendship breaks up. Maybe you're left bewildered in the friendship's wake, paralyzed to move forward. After wading through several difficult friendships, Mary DeMuth reveals the seven different types of toxic relationships and empowers you to identify the messiest relationships causing you the greatest anguish.

To learn more about Mary DeMuth
or to read sample chapters, visit our website at:
www.harvesthousepublishers.com

HARVEST HOUSE PUBLISHERS
EUGENE, OREGON